W9-BMW-226

Elephants in Your Mailbox

ELEPHANTS
IN

How I Learned the Secrets of
Mail-Order Marketing
Despite Having Made

A Truman Talley Book
Times BOOKS

YOUR
MAILBOX

25 Horrendous Mistakes

ROGER HORCHOW

EDITED BY A. C. GREENE

Published by Truman Talley Books • Times Books, a division
of Quadrangle/The New York Times Book Co., Inc.
Three Park Avenue, New York, N.Y. 10016

Published simultaneously in Canada by
Fitzhenry & Whiteside, Ltd., Toronto.

Copyright © 1980 by Roger Horchow and A. C. Greene

All rights reserved. No part of this book may be reproduced
in any form or by any electronic or mechanical means
including information storage and retrieval systems without
permission in writing from the publisher, except by a
reviewer who may quote brief passages in a review.

Library of Congress Cataloging in Publication Data

Horchow, Roger.
Elephants in your mailbox.

Includes index.
"A Truman Talley book."
1. Horchow Collection (Firm)
2. Mail-order business—Texas—Dallas.
I. Greene, A. C., 1923–   II. Title.
HF5467.H67H67   1980   658.8'72   79-19337
ISBN 0-8129-0891-0

Manufactured in the United States of America

Dedicated to my favorite Horchow Collection

Beatrice and Reuben

Carolyn, Regen, Elizabeth, and Sally

Acknowledgments

BECAUSE MY FRIEND
Stanley Marcus urged me to tell this story and prodded me
when I procrastinated, he has my sincere thanks.

It would not have been possible to write this book without
the dedicated help of the many people who've worked with me
in building the Horchow Collection into the successful operation it is today.

I'm also indebted to the loyal customers who have shown me
where my best mistakes have been made. To them I owe my
continuing education in the fascinating world of mail-order
buying and merchandising.

The lion's share of thanks and appreciation go to A. C.
Greene, who spurred me on to finish the book so many of my
friends had urged me to produce. A distinguished writer and
journalist, he spent untold hours transcribing, organizing, re-
writing, and editing the material I have been accumulating and
digesting since childhood. Without his skillful help I wonder
indeed if this book would have been born.

ROGER HORCHOW
April 1980

Contents

CONTENTS

Elephants in Your Mailbox

I

Suddenly, the Buck Stopped Here

EVERYTHING LOOKED the same as it had when I drove away that morning. The exterior of the building stretched off to my left for a city block, with nothing disturbed or replaced to indicate that a change had taken place within.

The same small black-and-white sign warned that double-parked automobiles would be towed "at the owner's expense." For a moment I even fancied the same two vehicles were still double-parked in front of it. I made a mental note to talk to somebody about having the sign repainted, possibly yellow on black with a skull and crossbones to show we meant . . . to show *I* meant business.

I bounced up the front steps and pushed on the entrance door. It wouldn't budge. A terrifying uncertainty hit me: My God, we've closed our doors. What was wrong? I had opened this door a thousand times, every day for two years. I shoved harder. A girl from the switchboard appeared on the other side of the glass panel, looked at me with concern, and let me in. I had been trying to open the door the wrong way.

Inside was only the random clatter of daily routine. A couple of typewriters could be heard, the hum of some piece of office machinery came at irregular intervals, and a telephone rang. A young woman with several manila folders in her hand walked toward the creative department, her heels clicking an obbligato to the busy sounds. No one noticed I was standing there observing. How could everyone be so calm?

From my desk I could see most of the main office, and I took a quick inventory of the activities, glancing around the room, pausing at a doorway here and there: Everything inside looked the same as it had when I left four hours before.

The letters on my desk were addressed to me, Roger Horchow, but a crazy idea that none of the mail was for me wandered through my mind for an instant. I assured myself I was the same Roger Horchow those letter writers addressed; I was the same Roger Horchow who had left this desk and gone out that glass door earlier. This was the same office, with the same people, working at the same jobs. The month was still June, the year was still 1973, and we were still located on a commercial street at the northern edge of Dallas. Everything was the same.

But it wasn't. No matter how things looked or sounded, it was a different little world that surrounded me. It was still a place where thousands of colorful catalogues were mailed every few weeks, and where we received and processed hundreds of orders each day for the items we pictured and described in those catalogues.

It was still the place where more than a hundred individuals were busy packing boxes, dealing with vendors, or talking on the telephone with people from all over North America. Everyone—tapping at a typewriter, answering a telephone, walking

4

across the tile floor, sitting at those desks—was the very same person.

But I knew better; I knew that everything had changed in the past four hours and (by now) thirty minutes.

Someone from bookkeeping appeared at my office door and waved a piece of paper at me. "Mr. Horchow, could you sign this lease for us?" It was for a new postage machine. The lease represented a cost of $7,200, not an enormous sum, but enough to create in me a sudden, sobering perception: Both the lease and the check were in my name. I had never thought about owning a postage machine before, although this had been happening for years.

I handed the completed lease and check to a man who thanked me, excused himself, and walked out the front door. I found myself on the point of yelling for him to wait a minute. . . . *You have over seven-thousand bucks of my money. My money.*

Then it hit me. Now there was nobody anywhere in the world I could run to, no one in an office up in some tall tower, somewhere, whom I could ask or blame or pass things on to. Now, when I watched those people at work in the office, when I looked down the long exterior of the warehouse, everything I saw depended on me. Those hundred or more individuals working somewhere out of my sight, and all those coming and going across my field of vision, now depended on me to stay reasonably busy, to be reasonably happy, to keep their dependents, and themselves, clothed, fed, sheltered, educated, and healthy. The buck had stopped, as the saying goes, right here.

On the face of it, I was entitled to be afraid. I had just paid a million real dollars for a business which had, in two years of its corporate existence, lost $1 million a year. I had used all the money my wife and I had saved, I had gone to many of my close friends—Al Roberts my doctor, Barney Young my lawyer, Michael Schaenen my stockbroker—old friends from prep school days, my father-in-law and brother-in-law, and each had given me money that might never be seen again so that I could write a check for $1 million and have it clear the bank.

I realized that I owed somebody $1 million which would have to be earned one dollar at a time. I was both scared and confident that they would all get their money back, but at that moment I had little to show them as proof . . . and it was just then that the immensity of it all sank in. The gamble was only beginning, not winding up, with the payment of that million-dollar check. We still had a big sign over the door that read "Kenton," but I knew that a few months from now we had to climb up the ladder and take down that sign and put up a funny name like "Horchow." I used to be able to say, "Well, Kenton's on this lease . . ." or Kenton was this or that, and there had been some shadowy "they" and "them" I could hold in a kind of reserve. But I didn't have a contract anymore with an entity named the Kenton Corporation. From now on, "they" and "them" were spelled H-O-R-C-H-O-W.

However, the fears and bewilderments of that first private hour were nothing compared to the thrills of realization which began overtaking them. I finally had what I had been reaching for most of my life. Now I could prove to myself and everyone else that what I believed would work the way I projected it. I had an opportunity few people ever get: I could test my dreams.

It was a priceless moment, and I haven't gotten over it yet.

I had been in the mail-order catalogue business for a little over two years when I bought myself, so to speak, from Meshulam Riklis, the legendary financier. Riklis had taken over the catalogue's parent company, Kenton Corporation, a few months before. The Kenton Corporation was a conglomerate which had been put together by two friends of mine, Robert Kenmore and Gardiner Dutton, back in the 1960s. When they approached me with the idea of issuing a luxury-type catalogue, early in 1971, I had accepted the proposition almost immediately.

The Kenton Corporation at that time controlled several of the finest stores in America—names like Cartier, Mark Cross, Georg Jensen, Valentino, Ben Kahn—and a mail-order business involving these famous labels seemed like an extraordinary way to get into the field. I had been Vice-President of the Neiman–Marcus catalogue and mail-order department for two years, but I had just found out I would not be made head of the section as soon as I had been promised. In addition, Neiman–Marcus was not ready to make their catalogue operation fully independent from the store—which was a move I felt would open up a new kind of retailing.

At my insistence, the Kenton Collection, as we named the catalogue operation, was headquartered in Dallas, not New York. I had moved my family across the United States twice, and I vowed I would not do it again. Besides, Dallas, with its central location, was an ideal site for a mail-order company, I believed.

We issued the first Kenton Collection catalogue in May 1971, offering items from the five major retail entities controlled by the conglomerate. However, in signing the contract which created the mail-order division, I had seen to it that I had the right to find goods from outside the corporate umbrella, because a main tenet of my mail-sales philosophy was that a catalogue should be operated separately from the store and independently of store buyers. (I must admit that I had been told, in no uncertain terms, by some of America's biggest merchandisers that my tenet wasn't workable. I was amused when, a few months after I started an independent luxury catalogue, several of them got busy and began copying my book.)

The Kenton Collection was supposed to lose quite a bit of money its first year, and it did. It lost a million dollars, which

7

was the figure I warned the Kenton Corporation to expect. The second year the catalogue lost another million, which was a great deal *more* than I had projected, but I knew the reason. I accepted the blame for that big loss, but I also could see that in our third year we were almost sure to make money.

Meanwhile, for reasons other than the Kenton Collection's disappointing record, the Kenton Corporation itself was going deeper in debt. Finally, in the fall of 1972, it was taken over by Meshulam Riklis of the Rapid–American Corporation, and my friends Kenmore and Dutton were out. Riklis and his managers looked at the catalogue and called me to New York for a serious interrogation. I could see the whole two years going down the drain, despite my certainty about third-year profits.

My contract with the Kenton Corporation kept me from being sacrificed in the sale of the company, but the Riklis people looked on me as a drag on profits and were uncertain as to what to do with the Collection—kill it or keep it? There was a fairly quick market for the rest of the Kenton enterprises.

I was as uneasy about it as they were. I was having breakfast at the Yale Club of New York about the time things were starting to fall apart, and I saw a friend, Baker Duncan, of Houston, across the dining room. I visited with him, letting my hair down about the mess I was in. Part of the mess, I explained, was that, *believe it or not*, there was no way we wouldn't make money the following year, having eliminated a very costly advertising mistake and having liquidated a surplus inventory quite profitably.

A spark came into Duncan's eye. "In that case," he said, "why don't you buy yourself from Riklis?" I guess I looked stunned, because he grinned. "Buy the Kenton Collection. See if he won't sell it. I'll bet he jumps at the chance."

Baker Duncan was a senior partner in Rotan Mosle, one of the largest brokerage firms in Texas, and an old friend to boot, so his idea inspired me to have confidence in the possibility.

He said that he would be glad to help, and that he would like to be an investor himself, which really got me excited.

In Dallas I was discussing Duncan's idea at a small dinner party with Jim Clark, who was then president of Brookhollow National, a new, aggressive bank that was (like Jim) very ambitious. Jim assured me that if I could buy the Kenton Collection he could provide financing. This was said in a rather offhanded way, but a few days later I found myself in his office, with a Rotan Mosle representative, discussing the idea. Again, Jim Clark said that Brookhollow Bank stood ready to provide the financing, either by itself or through an overline of credit with a larger bank.

All this was new to me, and I had the usual awe of bankers or moneymen in general. I assumed if the president of a bank said he could lend you money to do something it was considered accomplished. I went forward joyously with plans to approach Riklis. If I had known on what shaky grounds I was bargaining . . . well, I don't suppose I would be telling about it now.

In New York, I was ushered into the office of Meshulam Riklis and all I could think of was something I remembered reading in a financial journal; that this man, not much older than I, earned $900,000 a year. But after a greeting and handshake we got right to business. Using Duncan's phrase I said, "I want to buy myself." Riklis, who knew how much the Kenton Collection had lost, and knew we had sold down the inventory, replied acidly, "What's there to buy?"

I could sense that Duncan had been right; he wanted to unload the catalogue. But getting it wasn't going to be that easy. Knowing I wanted to take over a loser made it seem like a winner. Riklis stalled and played with me a bit, pretending he could foresee a rosy profit picture—while at the same time hinting his best move undoubtedly would be just to scrap the whole thing. He was quite shrewd about seeing my intense personal involvement with the failure or success of the catalogue. Finally, he said he would sell, but strictly on his terms: $1 million in cash, with thirty days to raise it. No payout, no notes, no haggling. Oh, yes . . . and a license fee of 15 percent of the profits for the next five years. He claimed that was proof he believed in me. His price and his terms were slightly outrageous, and he knew it, but I accepted the deal.

My brother-in-law Eugene M. Pfeifer III, of Little Rock, devised the financial package. I had no money to speak of, but I hocked everything I could lay my hands on. Since Brookhollow Bank had agreed to a loan of $600,000, we would raise the remaining $400,000 privately.

I very quickly got over the fanciful notion it would just be a case of deciding who to let in. It turned out, as I mentioned, that my only investors were close friends and associates and family members, who took my word alone. We went to the bank with our part and said we were ready to go with the bank's $600,000 loan.

Then I learned something about banks and bankers. Our banker friend, so enthusiastic about supplying financing, wasn't able to offer the entire $600,000. Small banks just can't make such big loans to people like me who want to buy a business which is failing, even if the bank president says they will.

I believe I came closer to panic right then than I would ever come again. I could not see how I could meet the deadline Riklis had put on the $1-million sale price, and I knew if I went back and begged for an extension, he might increase the price. The board and officers of the bank met several more times and at the last minute a loan was arranged—but falling $80,000 short of the promised $600,000.

I called Baker Duncan in desperation, and he reassured me, saying Rotan Mosle would buy the remaining units. Naive as I was about financing, I had no idea the brokerage house would

demand a commission on the sale, in addition to owning founders' shares. However, my main objective was to own the company. Somehow, I would unscramble finances at a later date.
Thanks to Rotan Mosle, I had more participants than I
wanted, but I had my money.

When Meshulam Riklis and I came to our sales agreement in
January 1973, I assumed (again naively) the takeover date
would be February 1. That had been the deadline for raising
the purchase price. Jim Mabry (now treasurer of the Horchow
Collection) had been bookkeeper, comptroller, and fiscal VP
from the first day of the Kenton Collection—when the book-
keeping department was a checkbook. Jim did a lot of behind
the scenes work on the sale and, like me, thought our takeover
would be February 1. In fact, Jim carried a $1 million check
around with him for several days waiting to find out who to
give it to.

Then the lawyers got into the act and things began dragging
on and on, dragging Jim and me with them. On at least six occasions Jim came to me and said, "Write another million-dollar check. I had to tear the other one up." The closing date was
supposed to have been later in February, then April, then
May, then June 1, "for sure." I had hoped to be able to get
down to work immediately, putting into practice all the lessons
our first two years had taught us and doing it for the benefit of
our firm, not Kenton's. I wanted to leave most of the financial
details of the sale for Jim to take care of, feeling I had done as
much as I could, lining up commitments for the money. I
thought our takeover would be a matter of handing over the
check and signing a few documents in line with our agreed-on
terms.

But, as I said, it was not to be. Months began passing, with
legal minds in New York and Dallas trying to decide the fate
of Roger Horchow, friends, and company. In the meantime,

we operated in a sort of limbo because, while the Riklis people seemed to assume the Kenton Collection was ours, we couldn't run it that way because legally it wasn't.

So, by June 1, there had been every kind of delay and false start we could imagine (and a hundred we hadn't imagined) and I was virtually numb. I didn't believe any date that was told me. Word came that the deal would be closed, again for sure, on June 13, and everybody around me said, "Oh, dear . . . the thirteenth. That's bad luck. Make 'em put it off a day." But I said no to that. Three and thirteen have always been lucky for me. I was delighted with June 13.

But I was nervous, and when the morning of June 13 came, I wasn't at all sure about how lucky it was going to be. For one thing, not long before, a friend had asked to drop out of the financing, with a unit. It wasn't disastrous, but it wasn't a very happy omen. I paced behind the closed door of my office, waiting for another crisis to occur. My experiences with bankers and money, by now, had made me determined never to be unprepared for the unexpected in this transaction.

And the unexpected happened right away. The Kenton representative, in New York, overlooked the time difference between there and Dallas, where the closing was to take place, and he cut his schedule too close for comfort. We had to close the deal precisely on time because Riklis would not okay anything further until my check had cleared the Dallas bank and the verification had been received by his New York bank and he had been notified. Everything had to be timed beautifully: The Kenton man had to arrive from New York on time, had to be speeded to the lawyer's office in downtown Dallas, all the Horchow people had to be on time, and the signing itself (which I still assumed would be a matter of a dozen signatures) would have to go like clockwork so that the Kenton man could rush down to my bank, get the $1-million check cleared, wire

New York, and transfer that amount to Riklis's satisfaction before the New York bank's closing hour.

I kept asking anyone who would listen, "Do you think they will remember there's an hour's difference?" Everyone assured me, "Of course, Roger ... these men do this sort of thing every day." I don't need to tell you, I was right. Those men who did that sort of thing every day forgot. And nothing else went smoothly either. I apply Murphy's Law on such occasions: Everything that can go wrong will go wrong.

The Kenton representative had been off schedule reaching Dallas, and when I was finally called to come down, the event turned into a Keystone comedy. There was a wreck on the Dallas North Tollway (something which seldom happens) that slowed us to 10 miles-per-hour. Then, when we got downtown to the parking building, cars were stacked up out on the street with a policeman waving everybody on. I finally got a man to take my car and wait in line with it, and Carolyn, my wife, and I ran into the bank building to catch an elevator. We got the wrong one that only went to the twenty-second floor. We had to run over and wait for another one going on up to the forty-fourth, and when we got it, it didn't skip one stop. We burst into the lawyer's office only to discover our banker, Jim Clark, wasn't there. Nobody could start signing until he arrived. I spent the most jittery twenty minutes I ever spent. I knew, or hoped I knew, nothing terrible had happened to him ... but where was he? He knew this was the most important meeting of my life, how could he be so casual, so careless? He was furious, when he finally got there. He, too, had been waved away from the bank parking garage, but he had taken it personally (after all, he was a bank president, too) and had called the chairman of the board of the large bank demanding a parking space be found for him. (And it had been—although I made better time just having someone wait with my car.)

By now it was noon, far later than we had planned. Our lawyer said to proceed to the boardroom where everything "was out on the table," as he so casually put it. When Carolyn and Jim Mabry and I walked into that boardroom, we were stunned. Jim Mabry's mouth literally fell open. The table turned out to be about fifteen feet long and was covered, and I mean *covered*, with documents to be signed. There were at least 150 instruments laid out—releases, agreements, leases, transfers of account, tax identifications, settlement of claims, assumptions of liability, releases from liability, legal files, tax files, insurance files, worker compensation papers, "dba's"—all hungry for signatures, sometimes in half a dozen places. We all sat down and began signing line after line, paper after paper. Someone peered in the door and asked if we wanted to send out for sandwiches, but I said not for me, thank you. I couldn't have eaten a bite, my stomach was so fluttery.

It took us nearly three hours to sign everything, and it wore me out. After about the hundredth time you do it, signing your name becomes an act similar to lifting a 50-pound barbell. The letters in your name become meaningless, and in fact, if you're not careful, you will begin misspelling your own name. The last thing we did was to hand over the $1-million check. The Kenton man stood up, stretched, and said he'd better go on down to the Dallas bank and get the check cleared so the New York bank could be wired before the close of the business day there.

I said, "Don't forget, there's an hour's difference between here and New York."

"I learned my lesson," he said. "My secretary forgot it's an hour *earlier* here."

"Well," I said, looking at my wristwatch, "don't forget it's an hour *later* in New York."

He looked stricken. "Oh, my God, I did forget," he exclaimed, and sprinted from the office.

The check cleared, the New York bank was notified, and they got the word to Riklis. I have that canceled check for $1 million displayed in my office—my favorite of all the hand-made objects that decorate the place.

II

Things Begin With a Stack of Dream Books

WHEN I WAS SEVEN years old, I spent hours and hours at my grandfather's kitchen table looking through the wonderful catalogues that came to his home in Zanesville, Ohio. It was like owning Aladdin's lamp. All I had to do was open one of those magic books and every toy I ever wanted or had thought of was mine—fire trucks, tool chests, bicycles, clowns, electric trains on miles of track with lights in the cars and whistles on the locomotives.

I think my fascination with the mail-order business began there at that old enamel-top table. I knew nothing about the organization behind the pictures, the care that went into each line of copy, the decision-making, the choices, or the sheer time invested in books with names like Sears, Roebuck, Montgomery Ward, Spiegel's, and Marshall Field. They were simply dream machines to me, wonderful dream machines, endlessly capable of taking me far away from that little kitchen.

That's when I decided, back then in the thirties, that I wanted to be part of that magic world of the catalogues. There was a natural interest in earthly possessions, but I don't recall wanting to possess the things in the catalogues so much as I wanted the thrill of receiving them, being able to have them delivered right into my arms. I would pore over the catalogues and think how wonderful it would be to order *everything* I saw. To be truthful, I don't recall ordering anything, but I always wanted to be allowed to.

Unlike some children, I held onto my dazzlement. I gradually grew away from the pages of toys, skis and boots, and boys' paraphernalia. I began turning the pages to inspect the adult *treasures*. The catalogues taught me what diamonds and rubies were worth, the scale of values for something as variable as Swiss watches, the subtle difference between silk and other fabrics, the simple beauty of good porcelain. I was taught what fine perfumes smell like in words, how crystal catches the light, and many other facets of the term *quality*.

I still feel the way I did back then in Ohio. I can scarcely wait, when the buyers come back from overseas, to see what new items they've found for the Horchow Collection catalogue.

My grandfather, Simon Schwartz, lived in Zanesville but had a little store in Crooksville, about twenty miles to the south. He sold mostly notions, shoes, sewing materials, yard goods—I remember the bolts and bolts of calico stacked behind the long table where the cloth was pulled out and measured to be cut. At Christmas he stocked lots of mechanical toys, which he loved. Family members recall finding grandfather seated on the storeroom floor playing with some newly arrived wind-up toy, while customers wondered where he was. But the greatest asset of the store, as far as I was concerned, was a sort of loft where he kept his leftovers, particularly a stock of outdated shoes. I loved to be allowed to prowl through the old stuff (he had opened the store in 1894) that had stopped selling when fashions changed. I know this is where I developed some of my love for old things—but maybe it's also where I began to perceive the need for inventory controls.

Grandfather Schwartz had come to America in 1885 from Bartfeld, a village in what was then part of the Austro–Hungarian Empire. He started out as a pack peddler, lugging his stock on his back as he went through the countryside, until he had enough saved to open his own store—a typical nineteenth-century immigrant story. Everyone in Crooksville seemed to know my mother and her sister, my Aunt Rena, because they had sometimes helped in the store when they were very young. The townspeople usually called me "Beatrice's little boy," even when they knew my name.

When the nearby potteries had a bad season, they laid off workers, and when workers were laid off, they couldn't buy from S. Schwartz General Store—which isn't very different from a city like Detroit and the manufacture of motor cars, just a question of scale. That, too, made an impression on me, because I used to think how bad it was to have things so tied up with one area and one industry. I believe that is one reason I wanted to have a business with customers throughout an entire nation rather than one which had to depend on an individual region. Incidentally, when I later became the china and glass buyer for Foley's in Houston, I was delighted to find myself buying china which was still being made by those potteries at Crooksville and Roseville.

You found all the Crooksville business district in a block or two. There was one of each kind of basic shop: A drugstore was next to my grandfather's store, and there was a hardware store close by, then a furniture store and a funeral parlor, and stores for food and feed and drink. There were offices for a doctor, a lawyer, and a dentist—most of whom I saw each day I was in Crooksville visiting the general store.

It was a marvelous experience for a boy, and today, when I read over a computer printout of our orders and find the names of villages and towns across North America, I remember little Crooksville and recall how it was the center of the world for me in those days, and I never think of small towns as "hick" towns, or as being "off in the sticks." A Farnhamsville, Iowa, a Featherville, Idaho, a Weed, New Mexico, or a Plains, Georgia, causes me to wonder what boy or girl may be living there who might someday be guiding and directing life for the rest of us.

Grandfather Schwartz was always alert to the strange ways numbers work—a trait I have inherited. He thought he had discovered that his life had been lived in a mysterious pattern of fours, and he once made me his List of Fours. Four articles had been his best moneymakers: red woolen underwear, boys' leather boots, womens' underwear, and ladies' hightop shoes. (Later I'll list my own best-sellers, but it won't include anything as fancy as red wool underwear—or as practical, knowing Ohio winters.) He had had four kinds of lighting in his store (kerosene, oil, gas, and electric); had used four kinds of transportation making the daily trip from Zanesville (train, electric interurban, bus, and automobile); and had sold to four generations of customers.

He closed the store in 1942, when his daughters persuaded him he had gotten too old to drive his own car back and forth, and when gasoline was being rationed as well.

Although I often think of myself as a small-town boy, from having spent so many happy days in Zanesville and Crooksville, I was born in Cincinnati and I lived the better part of my growing up years in Columbus, both good-sized cities.

I still have a warm feeling toward Cincinnati, as anyone does toward his birthplace, though we moved when I was seven years old. I remember well that we lived in a section called Avondale. Our house was the first one on Avon Drive. Back then it was like being in the country. The Hocks family—they still sell cars—lived on the street with us, and my playmate Billy Gradison lived nearby.

The Horchow side of my family came from Brody, then part of the Austrian Empire in that fought-over, ever-changing part of Central Europe called Galicia.

I was named for my grandfather, Samuel Horchow, but I never knew him, as he died before my father and mother were married. My grandmother Horchow lived in Portsmouth, Ohio, for decades, but she remained very Europeanized, returning to the Continent in style every year. She spoke six or seven languages.

My father was born in Portsmouth in 1895, the middle one of three brothers. They were very competitive with each other and were "stars," each in his own way. My dad enrolled at Yale in 1912. He was a brilliant student, earning his Phi Beta Kappa key and graduating at age twenty-one. Like his mother, he was a gifted linguist.

I believe coincidences all weave together in long strands in life. At Yale, my father roomed next door to Adam Gimbel, of the famed New York merchandising family, and a fellow named Bob Blum. When I went to Neiman–Marcus in 1960, I wound up working for Edward, one of the Marcus brothers, and unbeknownst to me then, Edward was married to Betty Blum, the same Bob Blum's daughter. Along the same lines, for years I have loved the music of the great American popular composers. Years after my father's death I discovered, reading Cole Porter's biography, that Porter (class of 1913) had lived in the same room at Yale, 31 Vanderbilt Hall, that my father (class of 1916) had. My father had gone into the Army as a second lieutenant in World War I. Then, because of his language ability, he served as secretary to Charles Seymour of the American delegation to the peace conference in Paris. (A third coincidence: Seymour was president of Yale when I attended.)

After the peace conference, my father was a member of the special Hoover Food and Relief Mission to Armenia. In those years of high-level globe-trotting, he decided to become a lawyer, so he returned to Ohio and enrolled in the University of Cincinnati law school. It was in Cincinnati that he met my mother, who was a student concert pianist at the Cincinnati Conservatory of Music. They were married in June 1926, and he went to work as a lawyer. I was born in Cincinnati on July 3, 1928.

My father practiced law until the early years of the Depression, and then, he used to say, although lawyers could have plenty of business, nobody could pay them. My father took a job with the Ohio state government and we moved to Columbus, the state capital.

In 1935 my mother and I spent a year in Zanesville, so she could take care of my grandmother, who was very sick. During that time, my father went to Washington, D.C., on a special assignment. I would go from my grandfather's house above Seventh Street and walk all the way through town to First Street and the famous "Y" bridge over the Muskingum River, so called because it divides into a Y in the middle of the river. It is still Zanesville's most famous tourist attraction, the only such bridge in the United States. I didn't realize, at the time, that lots of people came to Zanesville just to see that bridge. I thought it was my own private discovery.

During the time I lived there, some of the larger stores in town belonged to members of my grandmother's family. One very fancy store, Weber's, catered to the carriage trade. My mother's Uncle Louis Regen and his cousin David Weber merged their interests and had a wonderful department store named Regen–Weber where some of my cousins worked and, thus, where I felt right at home. One of my earliest memories, and something which turned out to be prophetic, was an occasion at age seven when I chose a gift for my parents' anniversary. I went to Regen–Weber equipped with hard-earned and long-saved pennies, nickels, and dimes wrapped in a handkerchief. One of my older cousins assisted me in looking for a gift, treating me just as though I were a valued adult customer.

I made her take out every single piece of glass from the display counter, and finally I settled on a French crystal ashtray which I thought was quite beautiful. It was a fortunate selection. My mother still has the ashtray today, and it would still be considered very lovely if unwrapped as a gift. But what became most important about the event was that it stands as my first independent choice of giftware buying. When family and friends exclaimed over the ashtray, it made my young heart glad and proud. Without knowing it, I had made at least a gesture toward my business future.

I don't suppose anybody consciously trains a child to become a buyer of fine merchandise. The thought never entered my mind. But the fascination of making choices, delivering them, then watching while the recipient enjoys them, was strong then and has remained strong in me. Once, when I was a little older and we were living in Columbus, I earned some money on my own and decided to buy a set of dishes for my family. I had heard them being advertised on the radio; you got an entire set, which was delivered instantly anywhere in town, for $3.99. One night, when my parents were out, I called the drugstore which advertised the dishes, ordered a set, paid the COD price, and had the table all laid when my parents returned. I remember that occasion as my first purchase of dishes. Many more dish purchases were to follow—years later when I was a china buyer for retail stores—but few were to match that radio-special set in my memory.

Other families had dogs, cats, a houseful of kids, or even a pony; we had our piano.

As I have mentioned, my mother was studying to be a concert pianist, and when she married, her wedding present from her parents was a beautiful Steinway semiconcert grand piano, which is in my living room right now. (Mother gave it to me after my father's death, when she moved into smaller quarters and didn't have room for the instrument.) This piano was always the central focus of home when I was growing up. In addition to her training in classical music, my mother loved popular songs, especially show tunes, and I can't remember a time when I could not hear, at some point in the day, the songs of composers like George Gershwin and Richard Rodgers floating through the house.

When it came time to move, the first question that had to be answered was whether the new living room would be big enough for mother's piano. A lot of houses we saw we weren't able to occupy, because they wouldn't comfortably house the family "pet." And, always, the piano was the big concern on moving day—the tremendous engineering feat of moving in and setting up this wonderful instrument, with mother supervising. It has a beautiful tone, and it contains the memories of three generations.

The piano led to a wonderful evening and an equally wonderful friendship, indirectly, after it came into my possession. In 1964, I was merchandise manager for the gift department of Neiman–Marcus in Dallas, and Dorothy (Mrs. Richard) Rodgers had written a new book about her home and her collections, titled *My Favorite Things*, which was taken from one of her husband's most successful songs. Neiman–Marcus was to introduce the book, and Dorothy Rodgers was to appear at the annual Dallas Book and Author luncheon. Her husband was coming to Texas with her. As head of the department which would feature the book, I was delighted to be told I would entertain Dorothy and Richard Rodgers in my home. The late Richard Rodgers was one of my absolute lifelong heroes, with his unbelievably long list of wonderful songs.

I immediately sent the Steinway out to be refinished, just in case Richard Rodgers might consent to play. The piano was gone six weeks, being carefully redone. But as things ended up, we didn't get to entertain the Rodgers; instead, Edward and Betty Marcus had a wonderful party for them in their home. Although I had planned for it to be my piano, and for Richard Rodgers to be at the keyboard, after dinner I was asked to play a few tunes, the Dallas people knowing my love for shows and my particular interest in Rodgers' music. I sat down and played a few of my personal Richard Rodgers' favorites, including a song called "Philadelphia, PA." When he heard me playing the song, Mr. Rodgers asked, in a startled voice, how I could possibly have known it since it had been cut from *South Pacific* in 1949 before the show reached Broadway, and had never been used in another.

The explanation, which was fairly simple, was another of those long strands of coincidence I have woven through my life. I had been at Yale when *South Pacific* previewed in New Haven, and I had been able to attend several rehearsals with a girl who knew Ezio Pinza's understudy—Pinza being the Metropolitan Opera basso who changed his entire career with his successful *South Pacific* role.

I heard the songs over and over, becoming familiar with them, and as I play by ear and don't need sheet music, I kept "Philadelphia, PA." in my head all those years. Although cut from the show, the tune remained one of my favorites. Mr. Rodgers told me it was one of his as well, and after that he took over the piano and played some of his own tunes, and told anecdotes about musical events in his life. He told us that the play *Evergreen*, which was a 1930 success in London, never got to the United States partly because one of his songs used in the play was considered too risqué. The song was "Dancing on the Ceiling," and the lyrics begin, "She dances overhead, on the ceiling near my bed." Some American producer thought this was too suggestive, so *Evergreen* stayed in England. The song is now one of the all-time great American popular classics. And Richard Rodgers and his wife became our friends, thanks to my piano—because I still consider *my* piano to have been the true center of the occasion that evening, although it was not the one being played.

III

I Didn't Follow in My Father's Footsteps

I DON'T REMEMBER ever being inclined to follow in my father's footsteps and become a lawyer. Maybe it was because his law career involved a certain amount of disappointment, but I believe the real reason was the character of the man himself, which kept me from feeling obligated to imitate his career. He was a very strong person, an intellectual who was guided by reason rather than by emotion or experience—which is the way the dictionary defines an intellectual. My mother complemented Dad with her warm, practical ways. Their influence was even stronger because they never made certain rules I was expected to follow nor made plans for my life. They simply insisted I do everything as well as I could, and let me realize they could be satisfied with my results as long as I tried my best; I was to be the judge.

This is a rule I have tried to carry into my business. All the people in the Horchow organization are encouraged to do their best and not care what the rest of the world is doing, whether it involves industry trends or something on the part of the competition. My buyers, for instance, don't worry about picking a loser from time to time, and they certainly don't worry about arguing with me over some item they want in the catalogue. I tell them my opinion is not law; *their best* is the only standard.

I started kindergarten and first grade in Cincinnati at the Bond Hill School, with Catherine Hynes as my first teacher. I entered the second grade in Zanesville at the Pioneer School with Virginia McFarland as my teacher. I fell in love with her, and when she married Mr. Bonifield of the hardware store, it broke my heart.

In the spring of 1936, when my grandmother died and my father's Washington assignment ended, we moved to Columbus. I loved Columbus, and when I think of "home," this is the place. I entered the third grade at Clintonville School, then went to fourth through sixth grade at Fair Avenue School. I attended Franklin Junior High, which gave me a twinge of literary pride, because James Thurber mentioned the Franklin Park section of Columbus in his famous short story, "The Day the Dam Broke."

Shortly after I started the eighth grade, we moved to Reynoldsburg on the east side of Columbus. In those days it was so far out in the country I had to take the county bus to get to Reynoldsburg School.

We lived on what amounted to a small farm, and I had a garden all my own, with fruit trees and chickens in addition to the seasonal vegetables I grew. I used my garden to help achieve Boy Scout merit badges as I worked my way up to Eagle Scout, a feat I am still quite proud of.

In the ninth grade I began writing for the local newspaper, a column called "Chatter From Reynoldsburg School." My pay was fifty cents a week, movie passes—and a byline. The experience didn't turn me into a journalist, but I began to see the exciting power of the press which lets the public see things and get information about things and, sometimes, motivates them toward doing things as a result. I am certain this exposure to the power of print formed the basis for a good many decisions I made many years later when I was entering the mail-order business. The little school column also gave me an identity and a distinction, ever so slight, from the rest of the students, which is very important for a child, especially when one is entering the teen-age years.

We were living in Reynoldsburg when Pearl Harbor was attacked on December 7, 1941. My father responded like an old war horse. Even though he was in his forties, he stomped around the house that Sunday declaring he would serve his country again, by God! Monday he spent the entire day making telephone calls and sending telegrams to all his old Army friends or Yale classmates who might have connections in the services. When a captain's commission in the Army came through, he was like a kid. I don't think he cared how high he ranked, he just wanted to be in the war effort.

Mother and I moved to Washington in the summer of 1942, so we could be near my father. I went to Western High School, taking a bus from Arlington, Virginia, into the District. It was an exciting time for an adolescent, learning to live in the nation's capital with a war going on. Gasoline rationing came immediately, so my friend David Fulton and I rode bikes and hitchhiked, getting around to seeing all the capital's sights, as well as helping with the war effort. I took my role quite seriously and immediately started a victory garden behind our house in Arlington.

In the fall of 1942, I went away to the Hill School in Pottstown, Pennsylvania, for my final years of high school. I made some of my closest friendships there, people I continue to see, like Jim Brown, Charlie Lynch, Sandy Luyties, and Dan Toll, who lived in the same hall with me. Guthrie Speers was my roommate, and I worked with Bob Abernethy on the yearbook. A few years later when I went to Houston to work, the only Texans I knew were from my Hill School association: Edward Randall III, who as a senior was my "big brother," and Baker Duncan and his cousin from Fort Worth, Bert Honea Jr.— both part of the great Texas Higginbotham clan. In the summer of 1944, the school asked several boys if they would return early and work for the school; manpower was unobtainable otherwise. George Harkins and I volunteered, and labored for three weeks at 38 cents per hour.

Through those childhood years I must have been preparing some kind of philosophy of life for myself. I certainly developed my curiosity about what people liked, and I was fascinated by collections. Sending off for postage-stamp approvals (mounted selections you may pick from at home) may have been my first practical introduction to the mail-order business. Among my most serious collecting activities, however, was the accumulation of matchbook covers. I had them from all over the United States and quite a number of foreign countries. In 1939, when I was eleven years old, I wrote a little article about matchbook-cover collecting which I sent off to *Childlife* magazine, and the editor published it in the form of a letter. That was the first time I saw my name in print.

One of the things I loved most as a child (and this, too, remains an important influence on my life and career) was to go to the Ohio State Fair in Columbus. I loved to go wandering through the various stalls of animals in the agricultural shows, and I never got tired of looking at displays—even things like home canning and preserving. In my boyhood scrapbook there is a newspaper feature story about my pals and me spending entire days at the State Fair, gathering up pamphlets, samples, and information of all sorts.

This experience was probably instrumental in creating my continuing interest in trade fairs and all kinds of exhibitions, whether connected with my business or not. And wasn't this probably the foundation for my reliance on market research? After all, I collected thousands of pamphlets offered by exhibitors on all topics. My juvenile market research was also enlarged by my unchanging habit of going in and out of all kinds of retail stores. "Just looking, thank you," I told hundreds of salespersons and floor managers.

Even as a small child I was famous for my curiosity. I was aware of what other people had in their houses, what they used, and how they used things. I'm sure I made a nuisance of myself on this level, asking questions and making comments which undoubtedly sounded downright inquisitive in a little boy. (I wish I could say I outgrew the habit, but the truth is— as any hostess can tell you—I still enjoy seeing what other people do with things.) Later on, this would become what is probably the principal ingredient in my formula for the selection of merchandise for sale: Always think of who might use it and what it could be used for, whether purchased as a gift or for personal use. This occurred to me long before I considered merchandising as a career.

What lessons were accumulated, starting way back as a child looking at the catalogues in my grandfather's house? The basic lesson is that a pretty picture enhances the appeal of any item. But there is a reverse to that: As in my case, some people like to look at the catalogues but may not buy anything no matter how appealing it is on the page. But then, if you tempt them often enough with a lovely display, they will someday find something they want so much they will begin buying from you regularly.... I became a mail-order buyer long after I started looking through catalogues. So, the problem is to convert the fascinated looker to the regular buyer.

What happens to cause people to buy? We can know, in a general way: Something is useful, necessary, or compelling because of its beauty or price. But, ultimately, buying is a matter of exercising taste; your taste or the taste of someone you are buying for, or the taste of whoever is offering you the merchandise. Maybe the taste is in the matter of quality, maybe it is in the packaging, or maybe it is in some feature of simple, true beauty that lifts one particular item above the others. Taste, under these conditions, is the ultimate motive for buying.

Of course, today, with so many catalogues coming to our mailboxes, the first problem is the simple one of getting the recipients to keep your catalogue and not throw it away. The next problem is to try to get everyone to read it. But one major advantage of mail-order buying (and selling) is exclusiveness. Young Roger Horchow, age seven, was perhaps only interested in toys, but he memorized every toy and every price shown in the catalogues, and he realized he couldn't find a great many of them in his favorite local stores. So he gradually looked to the authority of the catalogues as the source of all good things—things not easily available elsewhere—and that's where catalogue buying all starts.

But even in the biggest cities in the nation, there is that problem of convenience. Somewhere in a vast city you might be able to buy almost anything which appears in a book—but who could ever find it all, climb all the stairs, ride all the trains, catch all the taxis, walk all the miles and miles it would involve? Bell Telephone has for years advertised its Yellow Pages with the sales advice, "Let your fingers do the walking." That would make a wonderful motto for the catalogue business.

* * *

As I mentioned before, all these important influences and impulses of growing up are much more easily seen now than they were then. For instance, one of the important events of my career was door-to-door selling, which I did for years. Just about every kid sold something door-to-door in those days, so the experience was not exactly unique to me. But it did prepare me to absorb lessons which were tremendously important at a later age.

First I sold flower seeds in the spring, bought by me from the W. Atlee Burpee Company, and after that came magazine routes: *The Saturday Evening Post, Liberty, Ladies' Home Journal,* and *Jack & Jill.* Then I had a newspaper route in Columbus, and as I became a stamp collector and ordered stamps by mail, I learned something about the attractive lessons of "free offer" and "no obligation." When I went to the Ohio State Fair, I registered for every sewing machine; bicycle; church organ; and trip to here, there, and the moon . . . and never won a thing!

So what could I have learned that might help later on? Plenty. The flower-seed experience taught me to learn my immediate market; I had bought some exotic pineapple seeds because the picture on the packet looked wonderful, just like the pineapples in a can that I liked so much. The problem was that pineapples, beautiful and tasty though they are, just don't grow in Columbus, Ohio. I was stuck with those seeds. I soon realized that what I didn't know about pineapples and Columbus, my potential customers did. So I learned market research early.

One year I sold Christmas seals and stickers in October and November. In those days kids were said to amass a fortune selling Christmas seals—"fortunes" were $5 or $10, perhaps. Again, my problem was ignorance of my market. When I knocked on the door of some folks who were Jewish, they weren't at all interested in buying Christmas seals since they didn't celebrate Christmas. So, the lesson was forced on me: Know your customers before you start out trying to sell them something. Know who they are, what they want, and *if* they want it.

From the magazine route I learned a valuable general lesson of life. That is, you sure have to sell a lot of magazines to get those seductive, glorious bonus coupons enabling you to "buy" from the publishing company catalogue and cash in on a great new bicycle or some other longed-for item. I also learned, as I dragged from one door to the next, that you can't sell *Jack & Jill* to a house where there are no kids unless you figure out ahead of time that the customer has a grandchild or some other child to whom the magazine might be given. (And I also learned something about competition—that a great many kids my age were also selling magazines, so that even if a household contained children, you didn't always score.)

Of course, if you apply lots of logic and reason to selling, even as a youngster, you can quickly figure out a few rather surprising, and pleasing, things. When you think it over, you discover there is hardly any product that someone can't find a recipient for. If you can figure out who that recipient is, you have become an advanced salesman. I wasn't selling in the best market; it was in the late thirties and middle forties when the Depression was barely over and people just didn't have a lot of money to spend on the extras of their lives. So when it came time to sell *Ladies' Home Journal* or *The Saturday Evening Post*, you had to have a good reason to convince the potential customer to buy your magazines. I began to try to figure out what there was about this particular issue of each magazine that might appeal to the household on which I was calling.

The old ladies in their chenille bathrobes who answered the doorbell were told immediately that this issue had a terrific article on fixing your clothes and redoing your house at almost no cost. How-to money savers were big in those days, and I learned to capitalize on those needs. Most people didn't have much cash, so you had to give them reasons for buying that didn't involve much extra money, and, certainly, buying a magazine didn't cost much if it was going to save you a lot. The lesson: Figure out why people will buy things, what might interest them, what they might object to; and try to overcome these objections. Also, I discovered: A bargain, to be a bargain, must be useful.

All of these lessons in selling are very much the same in catalogue sales as they are in door-to-door. You have to be quick and to the point and very specific when you sell by catalogue because, just like the cute little boy at the door, you don't have much time to get your message across. The mail-order customer has an even quicker chance to throw away the catalogue than the housewife does to slam the door before the little boy gets to tell his story which motivates the customer to buy.

So, by the age of fourteen, I had learned, without really knowing it, most of the techniques for motivating the customer. What makes someone buy? You have to appeal to a real or imagined need, then close in with a product for that need—a magazine, Christmas seals, flower seeds, or whatever. And I learned that if you once get people signed up for a magazine, it's a lot easier to keep them buying than if you have to resell and reinterest them each week.

When I was a little older, I sold newspapers on the street corner. What did I learn from that job? I learned two very important things that tie in with the other earlier lessons, so that all the experiences flow together in a selling stream. People may be busy and preoccupied with other interests, yet they have a certain predisposition to buy the paper because it is a link with the outside world; second, if I'm right there to hand one to them, it's convenient—more convenient than walking into the front yard to pick the paper up.

Of course, one sale doesn't build a paper route. Selling one paper on Saturday night because it has the latest scores may make you extra cash, but it doesn't accomplish what you want. And sending a catalogue through the mail and attracting the person's attention, even getting one sale from it, won't build a customer list. Everything must be aimed at making repeat sales, keeping the attention and making buying convenient, furnishing a continual link to a fresh world.

Today, when a Horchow customer is unhappy or dissatisfied, we don't just *try* to make things right, we *strive*. And the very last question we ask is: "Are you still going to be our customer?" If the answer isn't, "Yes," we don't stop.

Selling papers, running magazine routes, trying to turn Ohio into a pineapple paradise can teach you things like that.

IV

I Fall in Love
With Retailing

I WAS ALMOST SEVEN-
teen years old when I enrolled in Yale University as a pre-med-
ical student in June 1945, on an accelerated program set up to
help churn out MDs for Uncle Sam. You started right off with
six solid science subjects; it was obvious from the beginning I
was not destined to be a doctor because I didn't like chemistry
and zoology, and those were rather important for a medical
student. I remained in pre-med until after Christmas. Then,
by mutual consent, Yale and I parted company.

My father, who was home from the war, told me he thought
I should stay out of college and work a year—take time off "to
grow up." I really didn't want to take a year off. My bruised
ego demanded I jump in somewhere and restore my academic
reputation, but I recognized my father's wisdom—and besides,
he had been very understanding of my failure; as always, he
asked me only if I felt I had been doing the best I could.

After I had nursed my scholarly wounds for a while and discarded the brief notion of trying journalism, I decided it would be best to go back to Ohio and put some distance between me and the East Coast academic scene. I went to Cincinnati and stayed with my mother's best friends, Uncle Charles and Aunt Billie Hochstadter, while I worked in nearby Loveland at So-Lo Works, which produced the famous Totes line. Then I returned to Arlington and got a job at Garfinckels, the Washington department store—and discovered I loved retailing.

Working at So-Lo, I began to get a feel for what actually went into merchandise, how production and sales were tied together, and how imagination lifted some items above their competitors—Totes, at that time, was ahead of its field. The Garfinckels experience was even more direct, allowing me to put into practice some of the things I had unconsciously been collecting all my life—things like customer motivation, making choices, and helping other people get what they wanted so that they left the store happy. (It is ironic that I sold little boys' clothing and accessories, and now have three daughters.) Indeed, by the end of my "growing up" year I had grown up a great deal.

When I re-enrolled at Yale I was ready for it; no more attempting something my heart wasn't really in. This time I majored in sociology, which I discovered to be very much in keeping with my interests, because I still had my curiosity about people and what they like, social relationships, and the forms they take. In 1949, my junior year, I went back to Columbus and worked at the Lazarus store on its summer training squad. At first I stayed with Uncle Joe and Aunt Florence Horchow, then I stayed with Bob Lazarus, a Yale classmate, whose family ran the store. That was when I decided I would aim toward retailing as a career. Lazarus was a part of the Federated chain (was, in fact, the original Federated store), so I felt I would eventually want to work for that organization, because my Columbus summer had been so pleasant.

I also met a lot of people I had not known, although Columbus had been my home for so many years earlier. I spent a lot of time, that summer, in a unique suburb named Bexley, which is near the part of town where I grew up.

Eugenia Sheppard, the syndicated columnist, had come from Bexley some years before, as had Charlotte Curtis of *The New York Times*. In fact, I found the area and the people who lived there, or came from there, to be so fascinating that my major paper at Yale was titled, "The Social Stratification of Bexley."

When I returned to Yale that fall, I announced to my roommate, Michael J. Egan, that I had met a charming girl in Columbus named Donna Cole, and regardless of the fact that he was a Southerner from Savannah, Georgia, she would be a perfect wife for him. I introduced them soon after that, and a year later they were married, and are still married. Despite being a Republican, he was the Associate Attorney General of the United States during the Carter administration. In fact, Mike Egan introduced me to Jimmy Carter well before Carter became president. In 1974, I happened to spend the night in Atlanta with the Egans when Mike was serving as a Republican in the Georgia House of Representatives. Carter was governor and Mike said we had a lot in common. "He's the only man I know besides you who has known exactly what he wanted to do since I met him. He wants to be President of the United States. I think you ought to meet him."

Not long after that I received a call from Plains, Georgia, and it was Rosalynn Carter. She said her husband had to get on the Texas Presidential ballot but it cost $5,000 to file, and the Carter campaign (then confined almost completely to Georgia) didn't have that kind of money. I told her that, based on what my Republican friend Mike Egan had told me about

Jimmy Carter, I'd see about raising that money. I helped, and Jimmy Carter got on the Texas ballot, and by the time the voters went to the polls, he had become strong enough to take the state. I was certainly one of his earliest Texas supporters—thanks to a Republican.

A few years later, when I was invited to the White House for a concert by Leontyne Price, I had an amusing experience. Rosalynn Carter, seeing me coming through the receiving line, called out, "Oh, Roger, we *love* your catalogue."

Could anyone doubt my pleasure at that?

I will refrain from making comparisons between Yale and other fine schools, but going to college there gave me the doubly useful kind of education I needed: My academic studies uncovered new directions and expanded ideas for me, while my social education included plenty of New York weekends and lots and lots of Broadway and New Haven theatrical doings. Yale gave me, also, a world of friendships I still treasure.

My years on campus embraced the period of William F. Buckley's *God and Man at Yale* (he wrote about all my professors) and my classmates included such interesting people as Robert Massie, Peter Matthiessen, Claes Oldenburg, Tom Guinzburg, John Crosby, Patton Campbell, and Jim Symington. Two especially close friends became important in government in later years: Bill Henry, who headed the Federal Communications Commission, and Larry McQuade, Assistant Secretary of Commerce under President Kennedy. Larry was a member of my wedding party.

I am rather famous among my friends for finding someone I know regardless of where I am. On my first buying trip to China, before there was more than a handful of Americans in the People's Republic, the buyers and I got to the Peking hotel and found the lobby full of people who looked important but also looked Chinese.

One of the buyers said, "Okay, Roger, I guess you are going to see someone you know?"

Almost before I could answer, an elevator door opened and an American-looking man stepped out. "I know him," I said, but the buyers declared I was bluffing.

Next morning, the man was seated in the lobby and, with the buyers watching, I went to him and said, "You're Jonathan Sloat and we were in the class of 1950 at Yale."

His face lit up and he exclaimed, "Of course, you're Roger Horchow."

We were in Canton for a trade banquet, with over eight thousand persons in one great hall, but few Americans. We had not made reservations, so we had to take seats wherever they might be. I was taken by a Chinese host to a table with eight strangers and put in the only empty chair in that vast hall—next to a friend of many years, Erskine N. White Jr., a vice-president of Textron, and his wife, Lee.

While coincidence plays a role in chance encounters, keeping up with people has more to do with it. I *expect* to find people I know. I keep the threads of the people in my life: the relatives (I've discovered new ones since I've been in the mail-order business), schoolmates from first grade through Yale, people who've lived next door, people who've worked with me. . . . I keep track of everyone I can. Keeping up with people has meant a great deal to me as an adult because I moved around so much as a child. I think from my earliest years I looked for some sort of roots. I couldn't get them from places or things, so I have found them in people.

People order from the catalogue and leave word, "Say hello to Roger; haven't seen him in years," or, "Ask him if he's the same Roger Horchow who lived on Bryden Road," or, "Ask him if he remembers the time the squirrel bit Lee Johnson," or, directly, "Have you forgotten who Fred Tarbox is?" In that case I replied, "How could I forget my Scoutmaster of Troop

88 in Columbus?" Many of these queries cause me to write letters and renew acquaintances after thirty or forty years.

I'm a sentimentalist and I look for opportunities to bring back, or share, happy times. Every summer my family and I spend a month on Nantucket Island and I delight in having as many people come by as I can persuade. And I take my family up to New Hampshire to spend a weekend with the family of my Hill School roommate, Guthrie Speers, at the exact place I spent my summers from ages thirteen to seventeen, on Squam Lake.

I'm a matchmaker, not usually in a romantic vein, as with Donna and Mike Egan, but in getting people and ideas together. I am constantly saying to someone, "Oh, you ought to meet so-and-so, you'd really like him," and it practically always works. I believe it's more than a happy trait, I think it's a gift.

My business also involves a certain amount of this same thing, because I'm bringing the person who needs it into the room, so to speak, with the merchandise. I have never been one to keep things a dark secret. I talk pretty openly about business. And because of this, I think I've run into a lot of helpful people who have shared ideas with me or have been incidentally helpful.

My office is located as close to the front door as I can get it so that nobody has to go wandering around looking for me. Some of my employees may think I'm much too available, because sometimes I end up with complaints that my customer-service sections thought had been taken care of. My people say, somewhat irked, "If a customer goes to Mr. Horchow, he always ends up saying, 'Yes.'"

Another trait that sometimes upsets associates is one of coming in with new enthusiasms I have picked up at cocktail parties or dinners. I know very well that one or two executives in the Horchow organization say, "If you want to sell something to Roger, catch him at a cocktail party."

41

I love surprises. I am, still, like a kid about surprises. But I don't like unpleasant discoveries. When discussing contracts or formal business ventures, especially those having an exciting potential, I always say, "Tell me all the *bad* things that can happen."

I've had people say, "Oh, Roger, you don't have to worry about that . . . that's not going to happen."

I tell them, "If it *can* happen, it *will* happen." The point is not so much to keep it from happening, but to be prepared for its happening whether it occurs or not.

Even though I was majoring in sociology at Yale, I continued to develop merchandising precepts and I began applying them when I could. For instance, at Yale I wrote for the annual. No one is really interested in what is *written* in a yearbook, they are interested in the pictures. After I had written the article, I asked myself, "Who is going to read this?" and I had to admit, very few people other than me. So, I decided that if you had to write something in what is basically a picture book, use names and catchy phrases to attract the eye. This translated itself into a lesson about display: Use big, easy-to-understand pictures and headings, or teaser lines, that turn casual lookers into readers. That doesn't seem like much to learn, but look at some of the catalogues and see how often this simple precept is violated.

I learned a lot about the relative values of others, too. What was luxury to me wasn't necessarily luxury to the next guy. I had three roommates and one, Wesley Dixon Jr., of Lake Forest, Illinois, was interested in the best of everything. Once a week he got a big bar of what was labeled "The World's Finest Chocolate" from the Union League Club of Chicago. My other roommates, Mike Egan and Dick Grave, were more interested in bargains. I learned, from Wes, that there is always an audience that will buy things through the mail, even from rather obscure sources, if the item has some distinct claim to their attention. That weekly chocolate bar was the first luxury mail-order sale I witnessed.

But that "World's Finest Chocolate" bar also taught me that even if someone doesn't usually buy "the best" sometimes he might splurge. Why? Because my two bargain-hunting roommates decided they had to have some of "The World's Finest Chocolate." They ordered a couple of the big bars for themselves, motivated, I'm sure, as much by the proud label as by sheer hunger for chocolate. So . . . never prejudge a customer's pocketbook.

I graduated from Yale with a Bachelor of Arts degree in 1950, knowing I would be going into the Army because the Korean War had begun. I enlisted in January 1951, choosing the Army because of my father's World War II career. I went to Armored Infantry basic training, then to Leadership School where I won an American Spirit of Honor medal, of which I am very proud. After I got my commission, I went to Army Intelligence School and was assigned to the Army Security Agency at Fort Devens, Massachusetts.

My work involved the analysis of large amounts of seemingly meaningless data—meaningless until I discovered the ultimate point of it all; then it became exciting. With my associates, it was made into a game, learning how it all fit together and trying to figure out why the data applied. I would take pieces of code or statistical information and try to see why they had come through, and where along the chain they might be used. I got a thrill out of piecing them all together.

We do most of that same thing today in the mail-order business. We, too, analyze input and results, we analyze inventory, analyze motivation, people, plans: Business today is as much analytical as it is operational, because the flow of information is so great that, to use it advantageously, you must know what you are looking for before you put your problem on the computer. I also learned, from Army code work, that nothing is meaningless, and if it appears to be meaningless, it can't remain meaningless.

So, the adage that no time is ever really wasted proved itself in my case. I tried not to let myself think of my three years in the Army as wasted, even though I concluded very early that I would not want to be a career officer. Even in my off-duty hours I learned things that came back to me later, when I turned to mail order. For instance, in watching my fellow soldiers buy posters, "girlie" pictures, and other items from the men's magazines, I began to understand something of that diverse market that exists outside of stores and shops. I couldn't help but notice what kinds of men bought what—and my company was democratically distributed along the social and economic scale. So, once again, the fact that there really is a customer for everything was driven home. And I still believe it, for literally everything. It's up to the "matchmaker" to put the customer in the same room with the merchandise and make a profit on it if he can.

Once we offered an exotic elephant ladder (used to mount the huge beasts) and had a genuine elephant in the catalogue illustration. We didn't have grand sales results on the ladder, but we got several inquiries about the elephant: Why hadn't we included its price?

A tongue-in-cheek letter writer said he knew why we didn't offer elephants for sale: "The problem is supply."

Our Customer Service director, getting in the spirit of things, replied, "The problem isn't supply. India's full of 'em. The problem is getting the elephants in your mailbox."

Of course, the matchmaker–merchandise–customer formula gets much tougher when you analyze who the customer is, what the merchandise is, and how and where to get them together—not to mention what you may charge for your pains.

Later, I will relate at some length the key factor in that formula, so far as mail-order business is concerned. It is such an important factor that it cost me $2 million to learn it—and took almost two years—and yet I will state it in one short sentence.

V

The First Thing I Had

to Learn

at Neiman–Marcus

MY SUMMER AS A
trainee at the Lazarus store in Columbus had convinced me I
wanted to go into retailing, and, further, that I wanted to go
with the Federated stores. I went to New York to be interviewed, and was introduced to Maurice (Mogie) Lazarus, a
cousin of my friends in Ohio. He was, at the time, Executive
Vice-President of Foley's, the Federated store in Houston.
Mogie took a personal interest in me, and even though I told
him I was going into the Army, he insisted he'd keep a job
open for me. The whole time I was on duty with Uncle Sam,
he sent me the Foley's store newspaper and we corresponded.

I got out of the U.S. Army a First Lieutenant in October
1953 and, after a few weeks at home, went to Texas, driving all
the way. I crossed the border from Arkansas into Texas at 3:13
P.M., Friday, November 13. I remember precisely because

my lucky numbers are three and thirteen and things divisible by three.

Lucky or not, I wasn't too impressed by that first look at Texas. I drove through pine forests to Houston, thinking I would find cowboys, cactus, and deserts, and found none, because the eastern side of Texas is lush and woodsy and not at all western. I went to work at Foley's on Monday and plunged directly to the basement stockroom. That was a sharp transition, from Company Commander to basement stockboy in one month, but, I told myself, nothing I would be assigned to do would ruffle me. Of course, Mogie Lazarus was somewhere upstairs in the Executive Suite. Not that he forgot me or disregarded my presence, but, in the real world, how could a senior executive of a big store like Foley's take time to run down to the basement to see if the new stockboy was happy?

But I was happy. Each morning I was assigned to a new department, and I found this exciting. If the department head wanted to keep me for a few days, I worked there "on requisition." Well, one day I was sent to the curtain department where there was a group of older ladies, and we got along well immediately. The younger buyer, Mary Ann Green, kept requisitioning me, and before long I was assigned to the curtain department as head of stock. There had been an opening, I found out, and the ladies were just seeing if a man would fit in.

My job was to make sure the curtains going on display were ironed and hung on racks, also to see that the stockroom was orderly, and to be available to help the salesladies bring merchandise to the customers. I remember that entire group with a great deal of fondness. I even remember their sales numbers: Mrs. Julia Aguillard (Miss Aggie) was 983/13, Miss Gladys was 983/2, and Miss Massey 983/7. Miss Aggie used to urge me, sweating over my ironing board, "Come on, honey . . . get those ruffles better. You know that four-inch ruffle takes a *hot* iron." They took care of the boy and he learned a lot from them. They were all seasoned pros.

I didn't mind in the least ironing curtains because I saw how important appearance was to selling—besides, I had learned to iron my uniforms in Army OCS. I also learned about colors—drapery and curtain colors in this case, but what I learned held true in most other lines. Putting up the boxes I discovered that *white* sold better than *pink* and *pink* sold better than *yellow,* and so on down the color chart. I also learned that the way merchandise reached the customer was part of the allure of the sale. If the box was crumpled or damaged, the customer would often refuse delivery because she thought the contents were damaged, too, without having opened the box.

How important is presentation? Now, when the Horchow Collection gets, say, seven hundred dresses from Mexico, all of them clean and tied in plastic bags, we send them out to be pressed, even though we will fold and repack them.

I remember my days at the Foley's ironing board doing curtains. Although I eventually went to other departments, the basement remained my favorite home at Foley's. When I left the store some years later, the curtain-department ladies sent me a huge farewell card and gave me a big party, down among the curtain stock. When I visited Foley's after I got married, I made my new wife go to the basement first thing and meet them all.

After my first year at Foley's, I was promoted to Stanley Blum's assistant in the china, glass, and decorative accessories department. Here, again, I was fortunate to be working with older women (and I still get cards from two or three of them). In the china department I learned about dishes from Mrs. Bruce (number 65/2). She said dishes were her babies, and they were for using. She used to take dishes and bang them against the counter and make them ring and say, "See? They won't break. You needn't be afraid of them." My eyes were opened to the sales potential for such relatively low-cost items as plates, cups, and saucers. I was in that department when modern plastic dishes were introduced, and I remember watching a table of them—dinner plate, cup, and saucer for $1—selling $10,000-worth in one day.

Later, as a buyer, I counted merchandise for reorder, and I began thinking to myself that we had to carry such a big inventory while the customers concentrated on buying certain items . . . what, exactly, did they buy and why? I always came to the same conclusion: Whether it was high priced or low, customers most often bought the things they could use or, if buying a gift, things the recipient could use. If we had an entire counter of glassware, decorative and useful mixed, the useful would always be bought first. Even in a line of decorative glass, like Venetian, the bowls and decanters sold earliest because a person could figure a use for them. Whenever advertisements were run on merchandise from our department, I tried to see that they featured something that attracted the customer because of immediate use. For example, glass corn-on-the-cob dishes would be instant hits when advertised during fresh corn season but languished on the shelf, even if pushed, during winter.

I still like china, glass, and gifts because that is the industry I worked in most. I like things made by hand and folk art. Sadly, there are fewer and fewer such things being made anywhere in the world. My office is decorated (or stacked) with handmade items I've found or others have found for me, from all over the world. I particularly like primitive things: toys, artwork, or decorative pieces that show innocent and honest joy in conception and creation.

I'm sorry there are so few such things that can be sold in a general catalogue. The problem is not sales—I suspect we could sell thousands—it is production. You simply can't get large enough quantities on any kind of complex handmade work. People often come to us with items, or concepts, that are quite attractive and salable, but they have no idea of how many of something we might need when they offer it to us. Sometimes they commit themselves to keeping us supplied, only to find themselves absolutely unable to do so. This was especially true during the first few issues of the Horchow Collection when we didn't know ourselves what tremendous response could be expected. A lady who made candy for us one Christmas had to be taken to the hospital when we sent her an order for five hundred more boxes after we had already reordered five hundred boxes the week before on top of an original order for five hundred boxes which she had been afraid to fill in the first place. We have a rule of thumb, that we expect a minimum sale of $7,000 retail on anything we put in a catalogue (it was $5,000 until inflation elevated it in 1978). This $7,000 figure applies rather well as a minimum limit, but there's no way we can be sure what the maximum will be unless we specify, in the catalogue, the number we have to be sold. When unlooked-for success comes, it can be more hectic than unlooked-for failure . . . and sometimes the difference in our hopeful estimate and customer response is staggering.

One of the worst examples of chaos of this sort involved some lovely old teak deck chairs from famous ocean liners. They were brassbound and had that marvelous patina of age and richness that appeals to us all. When we bought them, the supplier said to me, "They just don't exist, so you'd better tell me now how many you want."

At that point we didn't even know what the photograph would look like or how the chair might appear in the catalogue layout. That's the worst thing about our business: When we buy, it's so far in advance of even seeing how an item will look that we constantly have to gamble. In the case of a $295 chair, our rule of thumb at the time was that we might buy thirty chairs. But I reminded myself that if we sold out we couldn't get anymore, so I called the supplier and asked, "How many do you have, Jan?" She said she had sixty.

"What if we buy forty outright and you hold twenty?" I asked. She hesitated, and I argued, "The worst that can happen is that you're stuck with twenty chairs, and by that time you'll sell them to somebody else who will have seen them in our catalogue and loved them so much that we will have sold them for you even if we don't need them ourselves."

She sighed. "Okay, honey . . . just for you." This lady, Soovia Janis, is a character in the trade, a wonderful kind of old-time supplier from New York, who's just fabulous. She has an uncanny knack for finding great items, and I felt fairly secure with the forty–twenty split.

Well, the first thing that happened was that our Art Director, Vona McDonald, said, "It's fabulous," and put the chair all across a page—and the chair did look just wonderful. Then, the copywriter got inspired and pointed out all the glamor of this lost way of life, making it sound as if the chair had been on the ship as it sank and we dragged it out. Thus, the computer's first sales predictions, when about 10 percent of the estimated orders had been received, suggested we were going to sell not twenty, or forty, but 595 chairs.

I called Jan rather frantically and she said, "Listen, honey, I told you I had only sixty. You should have bought all sixty right then and had me looking around for more." She finally scrounged around and came up with a few more, but nowhere near enough to fill 595 orders. Who would have been able to predict that 595 people—in fact, we turned down more orders than that—would want a $295 deck chair from some ocean liners that had quit sailing? So, even with the computer, how can you win?

Today, we try to save our suppliers and ourselves from such grief, but it often disappoints suppliers when we say no to an

interesting piece of merchandise because we can see that production could never keep up with our demand.

Selling out quickly is one thing our customers can't understand. They call up and complain, "How can you be out of
this? I just got the catalogue." The answer is that orders came
in so fast our predictions didn't cover total demand. Our telephone operators are on duty twenty-four hours a day, seven
days a week, so two hundred items, for instance, can go very
fast. Also, our catalogues reach different parts of the country at
different times, although this isn't usually the major cause of
the problem. We almost always are back in stock within three
weeks, but on our one-of-a-kind pieces, subject to prior sale,
there's no place to get more. Even when we buy at a $15,000
retail sales level, we can't always predict correctly. In fact, very
high-priced items are the worst, when it comes to selling out
early. We once carried some very special rare enamel boxes,
offering only a dozen. A woman from New Mexico placed the
very first order and she bought seven of our twelve. The remaining five were sold within hours of that, so the entire offering was gone before a good many people got their catalogue.
Someone disappointed at not getting a box asked why we
hadn't bought more for the catalogue, but we explained that
the dozen was all that had been made.

We try to use experience, statistics, predictions, or luck to
outguess the odds; "hunching it" is the term we use, although
I shouldn't admit that we do, in this electronic age. We had a
$650 captain's chest (a locked, wooden case for wines and li-
quors) which we offered one spring. It was handmade by a
man from Nantucket whom I met on my annual sojourn on
the island, a beautiful piece of work. But how many captain's
chests at $650 do you think you can sell? The answer, really, is:
How many chests do you want to be stuck with if they *don't*
sell? So, after "hunching it" we said, well . . . how about eight?

That was $5,000 worth. We reasoned, if we can sell eight, or maybe six, we will have done our customers a favor and, at least, fulfilled an obligation to offer something special.

The Art Director loved the captain's chest, gave it a full page (hoping to sell eight sets)—and we immediately got orders for fifty. The catalogue hadn't been out a week when I called the man who made them and asked for fifty more. He screamed. "Fifty? How can you do this to me? I make these by hand, just me . . . I can't make fifty." We begged him, please, to try, and we told our customers we would hold their orders if they wanted the sets badly enough to wait for them. And, again, we had an unpredictable response. Every one of the persons whose order we were holding said, "We'll wait." Our maker of captain's chests heaved a giant sigh and went to work, and we finally were able to fill every order.

Then, in our wisdom, we said, well, if that was so good in a spring book, we'll rerun it at Christmas and repeat our success—after we are sure of a bigger supply. We reran it at Christmas—and sold about one-third as many sets. Apparently the people who liked $650 chests had already bought them. We were going to be stuck with several. So we called the maker and suggested he might have someone else he could sell them to. "Are you kidding . . . twenty of them?" he yelled. "No way." Which proves that in some cases, we're damned if we do and damned if we do it again.

On the other hand, the way I see it, this sort of guessing and waiting and missing predictions is a necessary part of our business. In order to offer certain unusual and delightful items, we simply have to guess. I would never want to have to sell only those products which are mass produced and offer no inventory or reorder problems, regardless of sales potential. I believe high quality and imagination are an integral part of mail-order merchandising.

* * *

Even after I was made a gift buyer at Foley's in Houston, I kept close to the customers. A buyer had to be on the selling floor from 11 A.M. to 2 P.M., and I liked waiting on the public anyway. I liked to get the public's opinions, although I never told anyone I had been the buyer for this or that particular item.

I learned just as much from criticism as from compliments. And when I sold, I never really thought about the size of the sale. At that time, in a store like Foley's, most of the sales were for less than $25, so *what* was bought and *why* customers bought it remained my two major concerns, not how big the sale might be. True, I did want to become a better salesman for Foley's, but I also retained that streak of curiosity—curiosity I think I would have had if I'd been working as a carpet salesman or repairing motorcycles. Even in my private life I still ask "Why?" at (sometimes) inconvenient intervals, and if I can't give myself a reasonably good answer, I know I'm heading in a dangerous direction.

I grew to love my work more and more and I grew to love Houston. Texas was a new experience for me and living in Texas imparts a vigor to life that makes living there distinctly unlike living in another place.

I believe there is no other place in the United States where a young, ambitious person can move toward his or her goal any more quickly than in Texas, especially if those ambitions are in a commercial field. Houston is a dynamic city, accepting newcomers quickly. I found myself at home almost immediately, and by the time I had lived there a year, I was on the debutante circuit—a bachelor with time to go to parties and with access to genial hosts and hostesses. As I mentioned, I knew only two Texans when I moved to the state, so my acceptance was not the result of social or business connections. Such families as the Weems, the Cabanne Smiths, the Bakers, the Randalls, the Lovetts, and the Browns simply made me a part of the scene. I have lived in Dallas too many years now to call myself anything but a Dallasite, but, despite the rivalry between the two Texas cities, I remain at least a *semi-*Houstonian.

I gained a lot of confidence in my career working at Foley's, and, in 1956, when Neiman–Marcus asked me to discuss employment with them (the family had just opened a new Houston store), I turned down the chance to join them because I felt I hadn't learned all I could at Foley's, and I felt I owed the store more time. But the offer from Neiman–Marcus made me feel pretty good, and I still have a letter from Stanley Marcus expressing disappointment that I would not be going to work for his store.

I was also growing up in other senses of the word. One reason I felt obligated to remain with Foley's longer was the sense of duty my father had tried to instill in me. I suppose he could be called old-fashioned today, because he put such emphasis on keeping one's word and staying with one's obligations whether they were enforced by legal contracts or not. My father died in 1958, and it stunned me with sorrow, but it also woke me to the fact that, from then on, everything I did would have to be based on my own experience and my own decisions. After working at the Pentagon, my father had gone to George Washington University and earned a Masters Degree in Business Administration in order to become a teacher. It was an ideal profession for him, and someday I hope to be able to teach, too.

A year or so after my father's death, I was discussing an order of china from a young manufacturer named Bob Block who was also a bachelor, and he said he had met a girl who was just perfect for me. "Unfortunately," he said, "she's engaged."

"Well, how could she be the perfect girl for me if she's engaged?" I asked.

A little later he said, "You know that girl I wanted you to meet? The perfect one for you? She's not engaged anymore."

So I said, "That's fine. Now I'll meet her."

It turned out to be a great deal more complicated than that. In the first place, the girl, who was an assistant fashion coordinator at Bloomingdale's, was in New York and I was in Houston. But fortune seemed determined to work things out.

I began to make buying trips to the big city, so my chances of meeting her were enhanced. But the girl, whom Bob said was from Little Rock and was named Carolyn Pfeifer, didn't necessarily want to meet me—or anybody else. She was still weary from the romance-gone-sour with the fellow she had been engaged to.

I really think that if it hadn't been for one tiny little coincidence, I might have given up even trying to meet this so-called perfect girl. But when I had been at Yale, going to the New Haven tryouts and the Broadway openings, one of the favorite shows that my friends and I had attended was *Gentlemen Prefer Blondes*, with Carol Channing. My fraternity brothers and I used to hang over the piano and sing the songs from that musical, and my favorite was "A Little Girl From Little Rock." So, when I had the chance to meet "a little girl from Little Rock," my dear old curiosity was so piqued I was determined to do it.

The first time I saw her I knew that Bob Block was right: This was the perfect girl for me. She was a stunningly beautiful willowy brunette, and very sure of herself, not to mention the fact that we shared experiences in retailing and department-store operation. I took her to dinner, but I wasn't at all sure she was impressed. I asked for as many dates in the future as I could, even though I didn't have any idea when I would be able to return to New York. But my work sent me more and more often to the East, and Carolyn and I found we liked each other. I knew I had involved myself deeply when we spotted a little dog being walked along Fifth Avenue, and she exclaimed, "I wish I had a poodle." Suddenly, getting her a poodle became the most important thing in my life—and I did it, to save my sanity. (Not that I liked poodles that much, or, as it turned out, not that Carolyn did, either.)

By June 1960, I began feeling bold. I sent Miss Pfeifer a telegram asking to take her to lunch on the thirteenth (numerology again). I flew up to New York and we went to the Palm Court in the Plaza, with its green plants everywhere, and violins adding romance. At that time we both smoked, and I very sneakily got her lighter out of her purse and hid it. Then, when we sat down, she began looking for her lighter to have a cigarette, getting madder and madder as she went through her purse. "Here," I said, handing her a box of penny matches. When she opened the box, there was an engagement ring.

I was grinning with pride, of course, and uttered that trite but magical phrase, "Will you marry me?" certain she would say yes, and fall in my arms. She did neither. She jumped up and ran to the ladies' room. (Two little ladies, such as are often found in the Palm Court, were sitting at a table near ours, and I had subconsciously listened to them as they commented on Carolyn and me. "Oh, he has a *ring* in the box!" one declared, then said, "Oh, he proposed!" and when Carolyn left my table, one of them almost cried, "Poor thing . . . she turned him down; should we ask him to join us?")

I told myself Carolyn was so delighted with my proposal she had to go shed tears of joy in private. I was wrong again. She ran to the ladies' room to use the telephone. She called Bob Block and demanded, "What in the world have you done? Roger has practically forced a ring on me, and I hardly know him." (I'll admit, we had had fewer than ten dates.) She came back to the table, quite composed, and turned me down. She wasn't ready to be engaged again, she liked the way her life was moving, and she didn't want to leave New York just yet.

I persisted. Commuting between Houston and New York, by August I had gotten her to invite me to Little Rock to meet her family. The evening of my first day there—after overhearing her grandfather tell some other family member over the phone, "Horchow? No, it's not Chinese"—I again tried to present my engagement ring—in a Band-Aid box. This time she said yes.

Carolyn went off to bed about 3 A.M. but I was too excited to go to bed, and I stayed up, moving from chair to chair, reading first one thing, then another. Carolyn's father, Eugene M. (Blue) Pfeifer, was an early riser, and appreciated this trait in others. I walked into the kitchen about 6 A.M. and he was seated in his robe, having a big glass of water (another of his early morning traits). He was delighted to see me, believing I was an early riser like he was, but I told him that, on the contrary, I hadn't been to bed.

"I asked Carolyn to marry me and she said yes," I informed him, adding, "I've been too excited to sleep."

Blue Pfeifer was so startled at the news that he slammed down his glass of water and shattered it.

We were married December 29, 1960. A few years later I had dinner with Carol Channing and I told her I credited her with my having married the girl I did, relating the "Little Girl From Little Rock" story. Miss Channing, who is one of the most charming women in the world, beamed.

Another important decision had to be made the summer of 1960. Neiman–Marcus again approached me about going to work for the store in Dallas. Even though I had lived in Texas for seven years and had been approached by the Marcuses earlier, I had never seen the flagship store in Dallas.

In August I made a date to be interviewed in Dallas on my way back from the East. I got in town a day early and slipped over to look at the legendary Neiman–Marcus establishment. I must admit I was overwhelmed, not as much by the merchandise as by the beauty of the operation. The housekeeping and presentation were fantastic. Subtly, the customer was made to feel the whole store was designed, and had opened its doors that morning, just for her. Of course, I was pretty cocky, so I found things to criticize. But there was one area I simply couldn't criticize, and that was the foreign merchandise. Foley's was—and is—a very good general department store, but did not, in those days, carry extensive lines of French, British, Italian, Oriental, or other exotic, foreign-made goods.

The next day I was interviewed by all the Marcus brothers in Mr. Stanley's executive office. An hour passed before we touched on such mundane topics as merchandising or my experience with Foley's. Stanley Marcus got the conversation onto European art, and my brashness allowed me to rush into my own theories on the Scandinavian influences on French Impressionist painters. All around me, as I spoke, were hanging fine paintings of the very sort we were discussing.

Foley's was a vigorous part of Federated Stores, and I was certain we were all to get great opportunities for promotion over the years. (As a matter of fact, Don Stone, a friend and fellow buyer who had a tiny office next to my tiny office in Foley's basement, went on to be chairman of Federated's Sanger–Harris stores in Dallas, a major retailing achievement.) As far as I was concerned, the glamor that surrounded Neiman–Marcus failed to make up for this.

But Stanley Marcus and his late brother, Edward, made telling points. They promised me a higher position within a year, disclosing inside-the-store changes scheduled, and Stanley, who I think is one of the world's greatest salesmen, sized up my career another way.

"If you stay at Federated, eventually you'll move," he told me. "Come here and raise a family, knowing you can progress in the organization without having to go back and forth across the nation." (Neiman–Marcus was family-owned then, with stores in only Dallas, Houston, and Forth Worth.)

My interview with the Marcus brothers took place during the same trip on which I had won Carolyn's hand, so I was suddenly thinking in family terms. The night following my interview I was guest of honor at a small party given by my only Dallas friends, Harry and Mimi Berkowitz, whom I had met in Houston. Harry was with Neiman–Marcus. The guests included Stanley's daughters, Wendy and Jerrie, and Jerrie's husband, Frederick Smith II, a down-easter from Portland, Maine. It was such a delightful evening I decided I wanted to be a part of the same scene. I accepted the Neiman–Marcus job on the basis that I would be quickly promoted if I were any good. I moved to Dallas and began working at the store for Ben Eisner.

I've always been glad that my first major move in retailing was to such an unusual store as Neiman–Marcus. Working there completely changed the course of my life, because, had I gone to another more commercial store, I would have become typical of the group of retail executives who move from store to store, climbing as they go but never knowing how long they will be allowed to settle down in any given city. That is one of the drawbacks to retail merchandising in the United States, which has to be accepted by anyone entering the field. Just about every major store in the country is now owned by one of the chains, and executives are moved on the basis of both personal abilities and store needs. In other words, the higher you rise, the more likely you are to be sent to another store that needs you, and once you have solved the problem, or possibly have shown your talents aren't what is needed, off you go again. There is never a stopping place until you retire. Of course, there were drawbacks to working for Neiman–Marcus, too, but, I must say, it took several years for the drawbacks to make themselves apparent to the extent that they began to outweigh the delights and advantages. There was only one store like Neiman–Marcus when I went to work there, and no other store in the world could have prepared me any better for what would someday be my chosen occupation.

The first thing I had to learn at Neiman–Marcus was the customer. Up to a certain point all customers are alike, but every store creates for itself a special customer who not only takes it for granted that the store will have certain brands or kinds of merchandise, but that the store can be depended on to have things no other store will have, things which this customer has learned from experience, or through the store's reputation, to look for. Neiman–Marcus certainly had its own customers, and it took a while for a buyer trained to think of another customer profile (*i.e.* Foley's) to accept this difference.

Not long after joining Neiman–Marcus I took a personal inventory of the gift department and took a list of three-year holdovers to Edward Marcus, the brother who was then general merchandise manager of the store. I pointed out to him that quite a chunk of inventory investment had apparently not moved well over a long period, and I went on and on about how much of it was what I rather derisively called, "hundred-dollar stuff." I wanted to put it all on sale, slashing the price and clearing it out. I'm afraid I acted rather high-handedly about the whole thing, but I really did have the store's good in mind.

Edward Marcus was a good-humored man with a great deal more patience about many topics than his older brother, Stanley. I'm sure if I had done the same thing with Stanley Marcus he would have answered me with a few short, direct orders that would have included the suggestion that I study my stock a little better, or think a little more about who "the Neiman–Marcus customer" was. But Edward listened and finally agreed I could move out all the "hundred-dollar stuff" I wanted to sell. (There was a lot of merit to my suggestion that the older inventory be pared down.) However, he pointed out, "Someday you're going to come to me and say, 'We need higher-priced stuff,' not, 'We need to get rid of this "hundred-dollar stuff." ' "

He was exactly right. Before many months passed, I could see that for a store like Neiman–Marcus—for "the Nei-man–Marcus customer"—the biggest problem was finding high-quality, expensive merchandise. It was easy to find things in the $10–$50 sales levels and you could always go in the other direction and get precious jewels that were unique but extremely high-priced. Finding the "hundred-dollar stuff" that your customers know they can't find other places—or know they can depend on your offering—is the daily secret.

Something else a successful buyer learns is a thing I might call universality. Buying is not all personal preference. Success is based on *editing*, making your selections so that you end up with that which serves the customer best. Many people suppose that being a store buyer is a matter of having "taste." Well, "taste" is impossible to define. After all, look how many things are sold daily which might positively *offend* a good many people if they were to receive them. And look at the tremendous number of things that are sold which do not involve "taste" at all. My only rule, so far as taste is concerned, is this: Never offer anything for sale you would be ashamed to give as a gift. When I am buying for the Horchow Collection, I always ask myself, "Now who would you give this to?" and if I can't come up with a name, I won't stock the merchandise. Someone might say, well, look at all the catalogues one sees full of utterly different things . . . and I reply, I don't expect to sell to everybody in the country, I don't expect everybody who gets our catalogues to want everything in them. But I do know (or the buyers know) someone who would like each item—at least, that's what I ask them to think about when they order.

And so far I've had an excellent record of success with my buyers.

When you're in the bazaar in India or in some Italian leather *bottega*, it all looks good. The problem is to edit, and that's where personal preference isn't to be avoided altogether. Sometimes you have special qualifications and can do customers a service. We have offered record albums in the Horchow Collection catalogues which I found simply because I like to prowl through music shops and record stores on Saturday mornings. Most of the albums have been on out-of-the-way labels, or have been repressings of shows or artists. My choices spring from my continuing interest in musical shows and composers, popular music, and jazz piano. I see albums even well-informed listeners don't know exist. I ask myself if I would like to have this album, and, if I like it, I'm not unique; even though I realize the market is limited, there must be thousands—a few thousand, at least, like me. So I save my customers the wear and tear of doing what I just did on Saturday.

While I'm discussing what makes a successful buyer, and such things as personal preference, I'll share an amusing travel disaster. A few years back I was determined to learn Italian. It would greatly assist me in buying in Italy, and it is a beautiful language. I also have always thought the Italians among the most fascinating people in Europe.

I bought several Berlitz records and immersed myself in Italian just before I embarked on a buying trip to Rome, Florence, and other centers of trade. I got to be fairly fluent, and, when a large group of buyers gathered in a small pottery district restaurant one night, I insisted I was going to order for everyone, in the native tongue. Since the district had few tourists, a familiarity with the Italian language was not only helpful, it was almost obligatory.

It happened that mushrooms were a specialty of this eating place, so, when the waiter came to our table to take orders, I addressed him fluently in Italian, announcing that the very first thing we wanted was mushrooms: "Mushrooms all around," I said, in Italian, waving an all-inclusive gesture over the table.

The waiter frowned, cocked his head, made a vague gesture, and repeated what I had said. "That's right, mushrooms all around," I insisted. Then he doubled over with laughter and we all looked puzzled.

From a nearby table a gentleman came over, apologizing in English, and said, "*Signor,* the word for mushrooms in Italian is *funghi.* You asked for *finòcchi.* In Italian slang, *finòcchio* is the word for homosexual."

I was mortified, although the buyers loved it, of course. And we did get mushrooms.

Our first daughter, Regen, was born December 26, 1961, having very considerately waited until Carolyn could have Christmas dinner before going to the hospital. That spring of 1962, Stanley Marcus asked me to go to the Orient with him and his wife, Billie, to begin preparations for the store's first Far Eastern Fortnight. Neiman–Marcus, as most of you probably know, has become famous for its annual Fortnights; two weeks in the fall when the Dallas headquarters store is almost literally transformed into a cultural and industrial outlet of some nation or region. As china, glass, and gift buyer, I would be especially involved in a Far Eastern Fortnight, because fashions and clothing would not be featured as much as they would be in, say, a French or British Fortnight.

I was delighted to be invited on the trip, and, knowing it would be especially pleasant for her at this point, I asked if I might take Carolyn along at my own expense. I was assured this would be fine with Mr. and Mrs. Marcus, so I rushed home to inform Carolyn, who pointed out that it would be a very costly vacation for her and subtly hinted that our budget—already accommodating a new child—might not stretch so far. I said then and believe now, you've got to do what you can do. They can take the house, or the car, or the jewelry away from you, but they can't take your memory or your experience.

In itself, traveling with Stanley Marcus is an adventure. Billie Marcus (who died in 1978) was, in her way, as adventuresome a traveling companion as her husband. It was impossible for anyone who knew Billie Marcus not to adore her wit, compassion, and spirit.

We arrived in Japan, the first time for any of us, and Stanley insisted we go Oriental, which consisted mainly of taking rooms in the Japanese section of the hotel and eating native foods when possible. Staying in the Japanese part of the hotel meant sleeping on tatami mats, which is, to a non-Japanese back, like sleeping on the bare floor. Sleep on the floor we did, for about three nights, then even Stanley Marcus surrendered.

But moving to the Western side of the hotel didn't solve all the conflicts of culture. The hotel workers were on strike, and we had to make up our beds, clean our rooms, help ourselves at breakfast, and, in general, be maids and bellhops. (It is no ordinary sight, I assure you, to see Stanley Marcus helping make the bed.) Somewhere Billie found some oranges (remember, this was before Japan had become so Americanized), and she insisted everyone have a certain number of segments each morning, "for your health." I can still see her, sitting in the hall between our rooms, doling out orange slices and making us eat them—making her husband eat them would be more correct, for Carolyn and I were delighted to have orange segments for breakfast.

His first visit to Japan had (I think) a slightly deflating effect on Stanley Marcus. We took it for granted that American and European vendors knew not only about Neiman-Marcus but about the Fortnights. We discovered it couldn't be taken for granted at all in Japan. We were in a silk manufacturer's office, trying to get some money to help pay for the Far Eastern Fortnight, and Stanley was going on and on about the celebrated luxury store—how much silk was sold and how famous the Fortnights were. The Japanese businessman shook his head in agreement, but Stanley never could get him to the point of our visit, which was financial commitment. Then it dawned on him that maybe the Japanese had not heard of the Fortnights. Cautiously he asked, and cautiously the man admitted he had not. Stanley suddenly read something else into the admission . . . had the man heard of Neiman-Marcus? The Japanese executive (not wanting Stanley to lose face, but seeing it was impossible to say yes anymore) shook his head sorrowfully, no. We "saved face," however, when, at the next place we went, not only did they know Neiman–Marcus, but the charming Japanese owner had on Neiman–Marcus shoes, which he took off to show us.

However, the surprise and the summit of that first visit came for me as we were walking down a street in Kyoto. Stanley, with no preliminaries, turned and announced I was to be Group Merchandise Director for Neiman–Marcus when we returned to the States. It was a very important position which, I knew, might eventually lead to a vice-presidency. To this day I'm not sure if he knew all along he was going to promote me, or if something I did on the trip put it in his mind. Maybe it was the neat way I made up beds.

VI

One Little Item Led to a Catalogue-Full

If I DO NOT REMEMBER the precise day I decided I wanted to go into mail order, I certainly can remember what merchandise started me in that direction. It was a glass dessert set, consisting of six plain plates and six bowls, and it sold for about $6.

When Carolyn and I got married, we received a surprise gift from my father's former boss in Ohio: one of the glass dessert sets. As we settled down to housekeeping, I noticed how often we used this lovely, unadorned set. It came out virtually every time someone was over. In fact, it was used more than anything we had received for a wedding gift.

Then, one night, we got brave enough to have Mrs. Herbert (Minnie) Marcus, Sr. as our guest for dinner. Minnie Marcus was a delightful woman who died in 1979 at age 97, widow of the founder of Neiman–Marcus and mother of the Marcus brothers.

As she left she remarked, "The dessert in those Steuben bowls was delicious." After she had departed, Carolyn and I wondered what she had meant by "Steuben bowls." Then it dawned on us, she meant our glass set. I decided right then, if Minnie Marcus thought those bowls and plates were Steuben, the set would probably meet the taste level of Neiman–Marcus.

I proceeded to buy 144 sets for test selling in the gift department. We put them on display and sold out in four days, so I knew this well-styled, useful item of good value would be a good seller. I reordered three gross of sets, ran an ad, and sold out within the week the ad appeared. Then I got bolder—and almost got fired.

I found out the freight to bring the dessert sets from Indiana to Dallas was disproportionately costly (the thick glass was extra heavy without being extra costly), and if you bought a rail-car load you saved a great deal of money—so the next thing I did was to order a rail-car load.

The car load arrived at the Neiman–Marcus warehouse (which is across Dallas from the store location), and, as there was no place to put this unexpected shipment, I was called over hurriedly. I told the warehousemen to stack the boxes along the main hallway, and we would find a better place later. Bill Bramley, who was the very austere and conservative treasurer of the store and was also in charge, generally, of the warehouse, came by, making his daily tour. He called for me and practically shoved me out to the hall.

"What are you going to do with these blankety-blank boxes?" he asked.

"I'm going to sell what's in them," I said.

"And what *is* in them?" he demanded.

"Dessert sets, sir. Good selling ones," I replied.

He almost exploded. "Who gave you permission to buy a *car load* of dessert sets?" Then he quickly fired off a burst of other questions: How did I know they would sell? Where did I plan to store them since it was obvious this was a lifetime supply? What would I do if they didn't sell? (That is, where would I get my next job?)

"You'll be giving them away," he predicted, and left me with a broad hint that I could forget my incentive bonuses for a year, if I survived that long.

Like the boy on the burning deck, I swore I would not abandon ship, that we would sell every set without reducing the price one penny, and that the long corridor of the warehouse presently filled with dessert sets would be empty within sixty days or I would resign or be fired, as he chose. I think anticipation of the latter caused him to accept my bluff.

I am happy to report the customers didn't let me down. In no time at all we were reordering another car load. We ran the set as a stock item in all the Neiman–Marcus mail catalogues, and it was established as a permanent stock item for the gift department, and, to the best of my knowledge, still is.

The dessert set story does not end there, however. When I started the Kenton Collection in 1971, I began carrying the same item successfully in the catalogue, and continued with it into the Horchow book. Over the years we have sold more than 100,000 sets, though the price is now closer to $16 than $6. It is the best-selling long-term item in the history of the Horchow Collection.

How did this glass dessert set lead me toward the mail-order business? Its success established my department at Neiman–Marcus as a leading producer of mail sales. Previous to that, I had not thought much about mail order except that it might draw people into the store who would buy from stock. But after my experiences with that glass set, I began finding other keys to mail-order success, and Edward Marcus, who was in charge of mail order, began calling me in to confer about various items. Later I was merchandise manager for cosmetics,

small leather goods, toys, china, glass, gifts, linens, the bedroom shop, and stationery, and, therefore, deeply involved in
all the nonapparel merchandise which would appear in the
catalogue.

I became fascinated with the buying habits of people who
bought by mail as contrasted with those who shopped in person. I learned that often the same person showed different
buying habits when using the two means of shopping. At Neiman–Marcus we had looseleaf mailers which went out every
few months, plus the famous Christmas catalogue. I learned
that sometimes merchandise which doesn't sell in person can
sell in a catalogue because you can describe its use or point out
what makes it different from something similar. To do this in
the store, you must have a salesperson right there, and have
the opportunity to get the customer's attention in the first
place. I also learned that there is some merchandise that must
be seen to sell; a picture doesn't do it justice. I became convinced that if we could only mail catalogues more often we
could sell much more, because (I believed) there must be
thousands of people who would love to shop at Neiman–Marcus but, for any number of reasons, could not get
there.

One other experience turned out to be a key one, although it
didn't relate directly to mail order. The first year I was at Neiman–Marcus I got a call from a man in Baltimore who said his
name was Thomas Hardie and he had the rights to a most
amazing new product—a skillet.

I told him, "We don't carry housewares," and he got a hurt
tone to his voice.

"I've walked a mile in the snow just to make this call," he
said, "because I was sure Neiman–Marcus would see the potential in what I have." He sighed and went on, "This isn't
just a skillet. It's lined with a wonderful new surface from
France, Teflon, and cooking foods won't stick to it." He had

the distribution rights to the United States, and Neiman–Marcus would be the first retailer in the country to offer
the Teflon skillet.

I was still not convinced, but I could picture him freezing
from the snow, so I told him to send us a sample. I gave it to
the late Helen Corbitt, then head of Neiman–Marcus food
service and nationally famous as a cookbook editor, and asked
her to try it out, but to be very "tough." Helen was hard to ex-
cite, but she came running to me after she tested the skillet
and pronounced it, "The greatest thing I ever saw!" She said
she was going to introduce it at her highly popular cooking
school, and, on the strength of Helen's recommendation, Edward Marcus decided we should run a half-page newspaper ad
when our shipment arrived. We did, and sold two thousand
skillets in a week from the ad alone. When Helen used the
Teflon skillet in her Zodiac Room cooking school, it started a
stampede. I don't believe I ever saw anything like it in Neiman–Marcus: Skillets were piled up, still in the shipping
crates, as in a discount house, with the salesladies handing
them out to customers like hotcakes at an Army breakfast.

What did this teach me about mail order? That *items* are
the way you make money. Mail order is *items*. A mail-order
catalogue should be a collection of *items*. Everything must
have independent appeal. Neiman–Marcus didn't have a housewares department, but did have fabulous success with a house-
ware *item* because it didn't need a whole line or set to make it
appealing. Mail order isn't a line, or pattern, in sheets or bath
towels; it is items. That lesson is one I have to teach myself
over and over, but it's worth it.

My years at Neiman–Marcus passed quickly and were always
enjoyable, but new thoughts began to emerge in my mind.
First, as long as I was with the store in Dallas I would always
be "that Neiman's buyer," or "a vice-president at Nei-

man–Marcus." My identity would always be tied to my job, and, I will frankly admit, I didn't like that. I didn't mind being identified with the store—in fact, I was proud to be an executive there—but I wanted something in addition. After all, my name wasn't Marcus. No matter how high I might climb in the store's ranks, I was *not* a member of the family. Someone named Marcus would always make the ultimate decisions—or turn down mine.

Then the Kennedy assassination in 1963 turned my attention to what I considered more human situations. From 1964 on, Carolyn and I were less and less happy with our Dallas lifestyle. I began to look for some effective outlet for political participation, some point at which my views would be taken more into account. Dallas, in the 1960s, was not such a place. Besides, I was growing through my thirties, and I had collected dozens of ideas—some vague, some concrete—about how retailing should be done. I wanted to try them out, and I felt I would never have the chance, working for someone else. I guess you could sum up my discontent with that classic American statement: I wanted to be my own boss. Then, there was a very practical consideration attached to whatever future I had at Neiman–Marcus. I had had no clothing experience, and in an establishment which depends so heavily on *haute couture* this fact means you must recognize your ceiling. Putting it all together, I decided to let it be known that I was available for another job.

I got a lot of response, but it came from other specialty stores, such as Dayton–Hudson of Minneapolis, and Stix-Baer–Fuller in St. Louis. I reluctantly passed on them. No, if I was going to stay in retail merchandising, I couldn't do any better than Neiman–Marcus. I wanted something new, a position in which my new ideas would be used and accepted—although I didn't dare express this to my interviewers, because I had no success model I could to use as an example. What I really wanted was to try a new approach to mail order, to separate mail order from store stock and from store buyers. This, you understand, was heresy in 1967. Mail order was accepted as an integral part of retailing, but it was viewed as, at best, a necessary adjunct, something "we have to do because if we don't *they* will." The mail-order catalogue, if there was a catalogue, and the department, if there was a department, were valued because of the exposure they gave store merchandise. They were thought of as something to bring customers into the store.

I didn't see mail order that way, but who was I, a mere vice-president, to be instructing corporations with decades of store-operation savvy about how to make money? I could see a new kind of mail-order book, one that used the store name merely as its entree, one that was not designed just as an adjunct but was its own reason for being.

Late in 1967, Peter Sprague, whose family owned the venerable Sprague Electric Company that pioneered electric street railways, contacted me and said he understood I might be available for something he thought would interest me. He had bought controlling interest in Design Research, a small but widely acclaimed firm of furniture and accessory importers in Cambridge, Massachusetts. (Marimekko was one of their discoveries.) He offered me the presidency of the firm, and I accepted.

Design Research was the brain child of architect Ben Thompson, who had established this avant-garde store because he thought new, good designs should be available to the general public outside architect-designer circles. He understood his customers perfectly and provided them with excitement and interest in the shopping experience, but his heart had remained with architecture, and, when Sprague bought control, Design Research had a bigger reputation than it had income.

Peter had hired me with the assurance that whatever I decided to do would be done. I knew it would be hard to improve on what Ben Thompson had established, and figured the only ways I could add to the operation (other than setting up certain store procedures and controls) might be in expansion into branch stores and mail-order sales. I thought the least investment, to begin with, would be a store catalogue as a means of getting mail-order business and as an advertising strategy for the Christmas season.

But, as it turned out, I hadn't asked enough questions when I took the job; I hadn't found out all the bad things that could happen. Although Peter Sprague owned eighty percent of the firm, Ben Thompson could approve or disapprove of anything in the store. He was completely insulated, acting as if he remained the sole owner, and disregarding me. I was totally thwarted. Thompson picked all the merchandise for the catalogue, and, I discovered, he didn't believe in mail order. No one connected with the operation would admit that mail-order experience from a store like Neiman–Marcus was translatable to Design Research. Any desire to make a catalogue succeed was altogether on my part. The photography was painfully slow, and this, coupled with Thompson's indifference, delayed the publication of the book until December 15. It didn't produce sales that late in the month, of course, and most of the Design Research staff shrugged and looked rather pleased.

Peter Sprague moved to oust Ben Thompson and give me complete control. The board meeting was called for a day in February 1969, and I was assured the guidance of the firm would be mine at the end of the meeting. That morning, when I arrived at the old house which was Design Research headquarters, I fleetingly noticed a man whom I did not know pacing up and down in the snow. I went on up to my office and a few minutes later Peter came in and asked, "Did you see that fellow out front when you got here?" I said I had but didn't know who he was. "That was the sheriff of Middlesex

County," Peter said, "and he served me with an injunction brought by Ben Thompson forbidding me to make any changes in control of the company."

Even though Peter Sprague actually owned most of Design Research, Ben Thompson was a Massachusetts resident, and it seemed to me he might therefore be more favorably viewed by the courts than the out-of-state Peter Sprague. Peter again assured me it surely would be just a matter of a few weeks before the injunction was lifted and I would be president in fact as well as name. But I believed differently and bet that the injunction would be in effect for a long time, tied up in the courts for at least a year. (As it turned out, the suit was not settled for more than two years.) I resigned that day. I not only couldn't fight that kind of battle, I didn't have all that much time to start my new career, so I was back on the job market less than twelve months after leaving Neiman–Marcus.

I started interviewing again, but, even though that winter was a pretty good time economically, there weren't many people who seemed interested in starting a mail-order business or backing a guy in it who had only retail experience. It was a dismal season for me and I was hurt in several ways. First, I was departing a job situation which I had thought would be exciting and rewarding, and I was coming out loser. Also, I had given up a fine association with Neiman–Marcus, a store which offered more satisfaction in its style of operation than any other I might go with. Finally, my first attempt to establish a mail-order business had been aborted before it had a chance to show me what I was doing right or wrong.

I crossed the nation to California and talked to the Bullocks people. I went to lunch with the top executives of Saks Fifth Avenue, who told me mail order would never be important in the carriage trade and assured me it was the thing they were least interested in. Later on, Saks expanded its catalogue, using the name "Folio Collection."

I thought a long time about whether to give up the idea of mail order and go back to working for a top store, or maybe attempting to raise the capital to finance some undertaking of my own. None of these avenues fitted my desires or made me happy to think about. But there was one facet of reality that kept nudging my consciousness: I needed an income.

On my way across the country that spring I stopped in Dallas to say hello to Stanley and Edward Marcus. Stanley invited me to lunch and I, of course, accepted. I was unprepared for what happened. He asked me to rejoin Neiman–Marcus.

Although leaving Neiman–Marcus had been unusually cordial, I knew there had been deep reserve on the part of Stanley Marcus at my departure, because, to him as to any president or chairman who has helped a young executive up the ladder, leaving smacked of betrayal and certainly indicated disloyalty. One reason I stopped in Dallas had been to dispel any cloud of doubt about our friendship that might hover over Neiman–Marcus. So, when Stanley asked me to return to the store, I was pleased and yet enormously surprised.

During the year I had been away from Neiman–Marcus, the company had been bought by Broadway Hale (now Carter–Hawley–Hale). The new ownership had agreed with Stanley and Edward's recommendation that the mail-order business of Neiman–Marcus should be considered separate from the store business; that it ought to have its own warehouse, buyers, inventory, and all that. It sounded like a dream come true to me. What could be better than to be in charge of something like that? Even though I wouldn't own my own business, I would be with a wonderful firm and have my career plans financed by others. The Marcuses and George Baylis, my former boss, assured me the Broadway Hale group would be very cooperative and I wouldn't have to worry about my decisions being countermanded from that source. I was tempted to accept the job on the spot, but there was one more possibility for my private mail-order dream which I wanted to pursue, so I asked for a month, and was given that option.

I have already mentioned that Bob Kenmore and Gardiner Dutton had formed the Kenton conglomerate (using half of each of their names) and were in the midst of acquiring businesses on the grand scale, from discount chains like Family Bargain Stores to varied high-end stores which, at the time, included Cartier and Mark Cross. They wanted to hire me to work with those upper-scale outlets, but said they were not particularly interested in mail order at the time—maybe in the future?

I spent a while living at the New York Yale Club and soon found I needed a home. Then I commuted from Larchmont for two weeks and decided, even more quickly, that I hated commuting. One morning I asked myself, "What are you waiting for?" I contacted Neiman–Marcus again to get the details straight, and it sounded fabulous. I would be reinstalled as a vice-president, this time in charge of mail order, a newly created position under the direction of Edward Marcus, who became chairman of the board. Edward would retire in two years, he said, and I would take over complete control of catalogues and mail order. I even thought I picked up a hint that I was now eligible to be president, even though my name wasn't Marcus.

Starting back to work for Neiman–Marcus, I enjoyed total immersion in the mail-order world, and I knew I had made the right choice by returning to Dallas. I began to learn things I hadn't been involved with before: clothing, and how it sold by mail; how difficult it was to sell costume jewelry (not very), and why better jewelry doesn't sell more easily (needs to be seen and touched). But the important lessons were the bedrock lessons I drew from experience because no one had set them down before.

As I have mentioned, I learned you cannot have store

buyers, with their specific interests and sales demands, responsible for catalogue buying. Catalogue buying is another world, unrelated (most times) to store activity and the demands for assortment of a store. In mail order the important thing is to pick out the items for your customers, to do the editing without causing them to have to do the going-through and selecting they do when they visit a store. As mail-order merchandise purchased by store buyers was presented, it became more and more evident to me that these buyers would always be geared to store sales—lines and assortments, not items. I was convinced the mail-order division would never touch its potential as long as this was true. I looked forward to the day when Edward Marcus retired and I took control. He was an easy man to work with, and he had many innovative ideas, but, from long years of training, he was basically store-oriented. He could never separate the two retail fields as dramatically as I wanted to.

I waited and learned, and, in 1971, two years after I had returned to Neiman–Marcus, I went to the Marcuses and said I didn't want to understudy any longer, that I had been told that in two years Edward would retire and I would take complete charge of mail order. I was ready. But Edward said he wasn't ready to step down yet. It might be another year or two before he wanted to retire—if then. Good friends though we were, I thought his decision—especially coming when it did—was unfair to me. My Kenton friends had again been pushing me to join them, telling me they were ready for a mail-order division. They now owned Cartier, Mark Cross, Valentino, Kenneth Jay Lane, Georg Jensen, Ben Kahn Furs, and Jacques Kaplan Furs. It made as impressive a list as anyone could want, so, with Neiman–Marcus changing their plans for me, I accepted the Kenton challenge.

The hardest thing I've ever done was to tell Stanley Marcus

I was leaving again. This time there was no happy farewell with going-away presents; the Marcuses were plenty mad, and the meeting was not pleasant at all. First, Stanley warned me I was making a mistake, that the Kenton Corporation was "in big trouble." "Besides," he said, not without a touch of haughtiness, "you don't know how to make money."

I tried to tell him and Edward that I didn't consider what I planned as being in competition with Neiman–Marcus, but they certainly did. Some time after I left, a rumor circulated that I had taken the Neiman–Marcus catalogue mailing list. In the first place, that would be almost impossible, but, regardless, the rumor was absolutely untrue. All I took from Neiman–Marcus was experience and good memories.

I am happy to say the gap in my friendship with the Marcuses closed rather quickly. I consider them among my close friends, from Stanley through his children and grandchildren. Before he died, Edward and I had long since patched up any rift in our relationship, and his widow, Betty, is a good friend. The Marcuses are aristocrats in the truest sense. They are never spiteful.

Stanley has left active participation in Neiman–Marcus, but the organization (headed now by his son, Richard) doesn't feel competitive with the Horchow Collection to any great extent. After all, mail order is only a part of the business, especially now that there are Neiman–Marcus stores across the United States.

Of course, I've never said I don't have ambitions. The first national publicity the Kenton catalogue got was in the October 1971 issue of *Business Week* magazine, an article titled, "Move over, Neiman–Marcus." As a Christmas present that year, my secretary had four blue finger towels embroidered with one word each from that title: *Move Over Neiman–Marcus.* The towels still decorate my office washroom. Some visitors, and journalists, have not known their origin and thought they were done as a challenge.

Well, they can be viewed any way one chooses, I suppose. Just so no one thinks they're crying towels.

VII

Success! At Minus Two-Million Dollars

THERE IS AN OLD POPU-
lar song which goes, "If I knew then what I know now . . . ,"
and, regardless of its grammatical flaws, the implication is true.
Had I known how much I had to learn I probably wouldn't
have started a mail-order business. There turned out to be so
many things I knew nothing about—things nobody knew
about—and learning them was done at heavy expense to my
company and my emotions.

Now, in addition to Regen and Elizabeth (Lizzie), we had
Sally, who had been born a few months before. So, when I was
approached to do a mail-order catalogue by a New York company, I said it had to be done in Dallas, I had to be the czar
(no second-guessers passing on my ideas), and I had to have all
the money I needed. "You're going to lose a million dollars the
first year," I warned Kenton, "the second year you may break

even . . . and the third year you'll *make* a million." We agreed on those terms.

Their idea had been to issue separate catalogues for each of the Kenton companies, but I sold the concept of one catalogue with a philosophy I called "Umbrella Shopping," so that the reader wouldn't have to shop several books (seven, in the case of the Kenton Corporation stores) in order to find two or three things to order.

Having sold the concept, I tried to think of a name which would express this "umbrella" plan. One night, in my living room in Dallas, my friend Emily Hexter thought of the name "collection." As she said, we were collecting all the good things in one basket; thus, the Kenton Collection was born in March 1971. In the past few years I wonder just how many dozens and dozens of times I've seen the name "Collection" used on catalogues? Well, we were the first, and Emily should be given credit for it.

Those beginning months were a synthesis of all the experiments and information I had filed or forgotten without realizing that someday they would have to be dredged up and made useful. There would be many friends along the years, and experiences that would pay rich dividends later—and many good deeds of those first years are still paying dividends. But I also learned a rather cynical proverb that grows truer with time. Sally Young, the wife of my good friend and attorney Barney Young, warned me, "Remember, Roger . . . no good deed goes unpunished!"

News of the formation of Kenton Mail Order and my appointment as president and chief executive officer was released February 23, 1971. In the press release, I pointed out that we were embarking on a new concept in the mail-order business.

"To my knowledge," I said, "there is no other self-contained mail-order business devoted exclusively to items for the affluent market, and I plan to offer merchandise from the Kenton subsidiaries and from other quality manufacturers worldwide."

I would not be confined to the Kenton firms in picking things to offer; I would expand where necessary into other categories, if the proper mix of merchandise was not available through a Kenton subsidiary. We then explored the idea of expanding into a wholesale division which would, in turn, supply the Kenton stores with new products that we could all sell profitably—and, at the same time we began the Collection, we hired Ralph Destino to create the wholesale division to develop products for all of us to sell.

Later in March 1971, I was appointed chief executive officer of Georg Jensen and went on the board along with Bob Kenmore and Gardiner Dutton when the Kenton Corporation took over the firm. But my tenure as head of Georg Jensen was brief and temporary from the beginning. As soon as I hired Tom Wendorff to be president of Georg Jensen, I was able to move back to the Kenton Collection full time.

Our first mailing was an eighteen-page catalogue sent to one million people. (That little mailer is now a rather nice collector's item, by the way.) The names were gathered from all the Kenton store lists of charge account customers and all the lists of friends of the Kenton Corporation, supplemented by names rented from various other lists available in the United States.

As you have probably read, there are lists of literally millions of names available in any category—professions, hobbies, incomes, cities, states, streets, ages, education levels—which can be rented by any mailer. We sat down and tried to reason out which names would be of most value in the new Kenton Collection mailings. We chose lists taken from social directories, lists of leaders of socially oriented clubs, of business leaders and prominent people where possible—and found we were entirely wrong. So, the first independent lesson I learned was this: There may be a correlation between wealth and the Social Register, but, if you're in the mail-order business, then pay attention to the mail-order customer, the proven buyer, not the rich or famous names.

Our best response to the first catalogue came from the original list of charge-account customers of the Kenton properties; in other words, people who were known purchasers. After that, our best response was from rented lists of known mail-order customers. In fact, the biggest surprise of all was that the lists of two relatively unknown firms—the Tog Shop, a terry-cloth manufacturer in Americus, Georgia, and the Amsterdam International company of upstate New York—turned out to be our most productive. That first mailing taught us the most important lesson one can learn in the actual operation of a mail-order firm—that any mail-order buyer is *by far* the best person to solicit, regardless of the fortune or prominence of other names one might collect. I can't overemphasize this point. The real, basic income flows from the lists of customers who have already shown experience with buying through the mail. That is why today the Horchow Collection's most treasured inventory is its list of certified buyers—Horchow buyers. One name on that list is worth a dozen names taken at random, no matter how highly placed they may be.

The original Kenton Collection catalogue, although mailed to one million persons, produced only 8,080 orders with an average sale of $35. We didn't make any money, but we weren't shocked.

We then came back in August with a slightly larger book of special items which would have to be ordered in advance for Christmas—for example, Christmas cards and things which take longer to get due to monogramming or engraving. This catalogue was also mailed to a million people, but our response only increased to about 12,000 orders. That meant, in mail-order lingo, a 1.2 response, which is highly unacceptable.

Although I had predicted we would lose big our first year, I could see that I was learning very little from this shotgun approach: firing wildly at a big target with what amounts to scattershot in hopes of bringing down *something*. I did realize quickly that we had mailed a lot of catalogues and spent a lot of money to get back very little revenue, so I was questioning the basic wisdom of mailing so many to get so few. But by then we had already printed a very fancy sixty-four-page First Kenton Collection Christmas catalogue and mailed the same million copies.

It was a smash hit. This time we received 40,000 orders, for a nice 4 percent, acceptable by the standards of the industry. Also, the average order, this time, was $40, so, with that Christmas catalogue, we were finally beginning to see the light of day.

Looking back, I suppose I did it wrong. If I had listened to all the advisors and list brokers that first year, I would not have mailed three million catalogues. I probably would have mailed only one Christmas catalogue, have mailed it to only a small number of "safe" names, and have started off 1972 with between 10,000 and 20,000 buyers, thus saving a lot of start-up money. But I wouldn't have had 40,000 good names to start our new year, and I wouldn't have learned that offbeat lists work at certain times of the year. For example, the Social Register lists didn't work earlier in 1971 but did very well at Christmas. We learned that certain lists were okay for us at Christmas even though not considered to be regular mail-order lists. The list brokers were amazed at our success with these offbeat lists, once we learned how to use them.

Sales for the first eight months of business were $2.3 million and we lost the predicted $1 million. Frankly, I'm still surprised Kenton stuck with us. I had predicted the Collection would lose about that, but I'm not sure everyone was prepared for it as a fact. But, at that point, the Kenton Corporation was riding high, in the winter of 1971, and it was apparent the mail-order section could succeed without losing much more.

The Corporation began an immense expansion. Fancy new offices were acquired and more money was spent on nonproductive things like art, elegant desks and furniture, and a limousine. And the secretaries started using the limousine to go to the beauty shop. I began filing away in my head a lesson which, unfortunately, did not last long. The lesson: Just because you have it now doesn't mean you have to spend it now. (Also, remember, I was not sharing all this beautiful nonproductive way of life because my office was in Dallas.)

All of which might well have changed my career—except for the fact that I made the first of my "Twenty-Five Best Mistakes" at that point.

Handsome headache—this $650 captain's chest sold so well the one-man maker had to give up. We returned dozens of orders because he simply could not craft enough of the cellerettes.

Nostalgia swamped us when we offered these old teak deck chairs from historic ocean liners at $295. Hoping for sixty orders, we had to turn down 500 when no more relics turned up.

Here's the glass dessert set that put me in the mail-order business. On an item basis, it's been our steadiest seller, with over 100,000 sets shipped.

Carolyn remembered a pansy ring her mother had, and when we found this one it was a big hit— even though we forgot to include description and price with the catalogue picture.

We got ahead of the U.S. market in 1972 when we offered these gifts from mainland China.

The Horchow Collection doesn't chase fashions. For example, this Halston Ultrasuede dress was being sold everywhere when we offered it in a 1975 catalogue. But we sold 600 dresses.

That lovely model is hiding one of my lovely Himalayan antique chests, for which I had high hopes. That may be why we didn't sell *any* chests—not one. The robe sold in the hundreds. The chest is my greatest buying failure, so far.

As an experiment we offered an original
Fleur Cowles limited series of lithographs
(this was the first)—and sold
the entire $700 series in two weeks.

For years Carolyn sought a useful,
decorative margarine tub, and this one
quickly became a catalogue standby.

Our famous ice cream scoop, with "antifreeze" handle,
keeps selling by the thousands each season.

◀ I thought someone was joking when it was proposed we include an 1890s feather duster in a 1970s catalogue, but modern housewives (and museums) have bought thousands, and it's still selling.

Daughter Regen found these colorful native bandanas during a Mexican vacation. We've sold 25,000 dozen and now commission our own designs in several patterns and colors.

A young American designer's career was suddenly enhanced when we sold thousands of these one-size-fits-all dresses. It also taught us that simple one-size clothing items are safest when it comes to mail-order sales.

This pumpkin-shaped leather ice bucket
achieved legendary status as a flop
because I overbought after meeting
its titled creator at a party.
The things wouldn't sell—
we couldn't even give 'em away.

Little Bunky Vroom didn't know his picture
in this rescue helmet with flashing light
would be a Horchow Classic.

Our Fornasetti hand-painted
faux-malachite plates had to be sold
as non–hand-painted ashtrays.

How could these darling velvet
dresses lose? By missing the Christmas
catalogue is how. They ended up
as gifts to a children's home.

A simply *classico* loser, this Italian hat-lamp. None of the buyers will admit to ordering this bummer (including me).

Bilston & Battersea porcelain boxes made for us to honor the American Institute for Public Service's Jefferson Awards.

Our title picture: We offered this $750 elephant ladder for use in the library. Nobody wanted the ladder; they wanted to know the price of the elephant instead.

These Texas wheeler-dealers include (clockwise from left)
Tino Vasquez; Dee Foley; Carolyn, Lizzie, and Sally Horchow;
a neighbor's shaggy dog; Owen and Luke Wilson;
and infrequent cyclist SRH. Our object was to
sell clothing—not including the shaggy dog's hat.

VIII

My Twenty-Five Best Mistakes

In THE YEARS SINCE I have been in the mail-order business I have been interviewed, have spoken to business schools, and have addressed sales conventions about my mistakes and my successes. I tend to be candid about both, and I have never felt it hurt to be as open about failure as about success—in fact, it's probably better to be candid about failures.

But, in doing this, I have created my own monster. I have made the business sound simple and the mistakes easy to overcome. The monster is the proliferation of catalogues nearly identical to mine. I entered an industry in 1971 and quickly did something no one else had done, but, instead of keeping quiet about it and just pushing the idea that we had a nice little catalogue, "and please buy from us," I allowed my publicity to spell out how successful and wonderful we were and how much money we were making. So, while Americans like success stories—and success promotes more success—I think I overdid it. People read articles about the Horchow organization and said to themselves, "I know enough about retailing to do what he did. He worked for Foley's and Neiman–Marcus, but I worked for so-and-so, which is as big a store as those are. . . . I've got good taste; I'll hire an art director and we'll join this mail-order paradise."

This gets more believable when you see as many catalogues as I do. Ninety percent of them have similar wording, or *identical* wording, to ours. Many have lifted the exact phrases we use in our informational memos. Several catalogues even use the same typeface as the Horchow Collection. Check for yourself.

As I was saying, I created my own monster because I made it seem easy to get into the mail-order business. Only, most get in and get out pretty fast. For a few years, somebody showed me a new luxury book every week, but then more began falling by the wayside than were springing up.

I started this chapter talking about mistakes, and I've gotten off into the perils of success. Mistakes are more fun to read about. I told a newspaper columnist a few years ago that I wanted to write a book about "My Twenty-Five Best Mistakes," and three publishers called or wrote me to say they'd like to see the manuscript when I did it. Well, the joke was on me. When I sat down to list my twenty-five best mistakes, I ended up with eighty-seven . . . at least, that's where I quit listing.

But, whether they number twenty-five or eighty-seven, the important thing about mistakes is, do you profit from them? Note that I referred to my *best* mistakes, not my *worst* mistakes. My *best* mistakes are the ones which caused me to change, even though it might have taken two or three repetitions to recognize my error. My *worst* mistakes are the ones I still don't know about.

One of my characteristics, on which I have already dwelt, is the fact that I keep up with friends from the past, even though I may not see them very often. This practice has not always served me in good stead, however. In the case I'm about to describe, I had kept up with M. from prep school, who, over the years, had gone from advertising to the business of selling educational courses by mail, and he and I used to have lunch occasionally when I was in New York. That winter of 1971, it occurred to me that M. must know a lot about building lists because he had done that for a very big mail-order and publishing firm.

Next time I was in New York we discussed my new company and talked about building up our list, and, before I knew it, I had hired him to become the manager of list expansion. Since he was an old school friend, I took for granted that anything he told me would be correct. M. announced that within a year he would increase our list by tens of thousands of names and would have added a million dollars in sales to our business. Since I had been urged to hire experts in fields about which I supposedly knew nothing, I was pleased to be able to hire an obvious expert who was also a friend.

A first big mistake: Never hire a friend . . . or, if that's too dogmatic, add Gilbert and Sullivan's qualifier, "well, *hardly* ever." At best, it is difficult to deal with friends if you don't agree with their actions, their decisions, or their projects. You tend to protect the friendship more than the business objectives.

We embarked on M.'s scheme for riches. He told us of many ways to get free space in magazines, based on the supposition that the magazine would put up empty (or unsold) space and we would give it a share of the profits from the ads it would carry—but that would work in our favor because we would pick up so many new names to add to our list.

M.'s marketing plan was to select a lot of merchandise which could be easily obtained during Christmas if we needed to reorder. From this easy-to-get merchandise we would pick goods we knew, from previous experience, sold well. Then we had to figure out a way to be able to handle all the orders we would get from our regular Christmas sales (and we expected this to run 80,000 orders, or double the previous season) and at the same time keep up with the fantastic magazine response we were going to get.

It hurts to tell this now, it's so easy to spot soft places in the plan. With high expectations we hired a separate warehouse and order fulfillment facility in Tempe, Arizona. We then hired several special people who would do nothing but deal with magazine orders, keeping the Arizona warehouse in stock at all times.

What happened was a nightmare. First, although the Arizona facility was very big and very efficient, we had not taken into account that they, as we, could make mistakes, and that customers wouldn't know that orders placed through the Kenton Collection in Arizona had a special customer service activity separate from the Kenton Collection in Dallas. We soon had all the customers from Arizona calling us in Dallas about their orders, but we didn't know what, where, or when about things in Arizona. In addition to the mechanical difficulties encountered in handling orders, there was the gnawing problem that we weren't selling enough merchandise, in most cases, to make any profit after paying for the ad.

Since the experiment was designed around merchandise we thought would sell well, we embarked on a series of large purchases. We were afraid that if we didn't buy the merchandise early there wouldn't be enough available by the time the special magazine orders came in—because the magazine orders were to be direct, from magazine readers who wouldn't have a Kenton Collection catalogue. For example, we had a $10 apron which we had sold through the catalogue in the thousands. With the magazine orders in mind, we bought 15,000 aprons, having to invest our money in advance to assure the supply from the vendor. We repeated this procedure with several items.

Once again, it was a disaster. We had terrible problems trying to keep our records straight, so far as deliveries from the manufacturers and orders from the customers were concerned. Everything we did in Dallas was made more difficult by the fact that the warehouse was in Arizona.

Our regular Kenton Collection catalogue business was going along very well, so far as we could tell from the confused picture of orders and deliveries. But the drain on our resources—buying inflated inventory, handling transfers of merchandise and trying to keep track of what we had in the other state—proved to be more than we could cope with. To put it bluntly: We weren't sure what we were supposed to be doing, or how things were supposed to be operating.

On top of all the confusion, because the whole thing was set up by a friend and I thought the details would be taken care of, I failed to read the fine print. As I understood the deal, we were to pay for the magazine ads from profits on the merchandise sold through that particular magazine. No one mentioned what would happen if there were not enough profits to pay for the ads. I had assumed (and it was naive of me, I'll admit) that the ad space provided by the various magazines was, in effect, free, in that the magazines always had extra space which had not sold and therefore they were glad to try our experiment. It turned out, when the chips were down, that we weren't really dealing with the magazines, but with an intermediary (or, in many cases, two intermediaries), who was not empowered to speak for the magazines. We ended up having to pay an arm and a leg to get out of all the various agreements, which I had thought involved free, or cost-proof, ad space. Our hopes for making any profit—or breaking even—in 1972 were long gone.

By the time this magazine fiasco had played its course, the entire Kenton conglomerate had been fully taken over by the Meshulam Riklis group of Rapid–American fame. The problems in the Kenton Corporation were separate from ours. All their big spending and expansion, which we had nothing to do with, forced the change. As a matter of fact, every time the Kenton Corporation had bought something new, I had bought something old. Everything in our office was secondhand. My desk is still an old one I first found in the Jensen warehouse during my brief chairmanship. So, in spite of our difficulties, it wasn't the Collection that collapsed the original Kenton Corporation's dreams.

In Dallas we were shell-shocked by our magazine disaster, and in New York the Corporation was being given the shock treatment by Riklis. First of all, my friends, the founders, left the company. Then the Riklis people turned a baleful eye on the Collection, as it was showing a million-dollar loss for the second year in a row. The first direct order I got from the new management was to fire everybody involved with the magazine advertising experiment, so I reluctantly fired my prep school friend—but I must say, in his defense, I believe he was really best as a marketing promoter, not as a list developer.

Another positive thing that came out of this purge was the insistence by the Riklis management that we liquidate inventory. We had never really considered the possibility of having large overstocks (one of the virtues of mail order is that you only stock enough to cover immediate sales), but suddenly we had them. This caused us to initiate our first Kenton Collection "Sale-by-Mail." To my surprise, it was an enormous success. We sold out of everything and lowered our inventory by almost a million dollars in just one month. This was a revelation amidst all the gloom: We could liquidate inventory at little loss. In fact, we pretty well broke even, including production cost of the "Sale-by-Mail" book. This lesson stood us in good stead at later times when we liquidated inventory, not from panic but as part of planned procedure.

I am sure there have been mail-order operations that have made a success of the kind of magazine advertising we tried, but what advantages we got were far offset by the complications involved. Another bitter lesson: Never put your customer-service facility in the hands of strangers, since customer service, above all other sections, represents your company most directly and most intimately. You must have complete control over it. To have a person in Tempe, Arizona, speaking on behalf of a company in Dallas, Texas, never having seen the company and having no knowledge of its principles, can quickly lead to extinction of the company.

Yet another lesson: Just because merchandise sells well through a catalogue, you can never assume the same merchandise will be equally attractive to persons thumbing through a popular magazine. One basis for our magazine ad program (other than my friend's enthusiasm) was the fact that we had, in January 1972, run some pages of best-selling catalogue items in the American Express magazine, *Travel and Leisure,* and achieved a good response. If we received good response in a January–February magazine, we reasoned, then doing the same thing in a number of magazines during the best-selling season of fall should at least triple results. We tried it, and the result came out disastrously: We did one-third the business in the fall we had done the winter before. Fine magazines, fine merchandise . . . what happened? The lesson: Just because you have performed one test, you don't have the freedom to generalize. An experiment must be validated more than once or it remains a gamble.

To be candid, if we had the whole experiment to do over again, based on our same original information, I suppose we might do the same thing; we might assume, as in the case of *Travel and Leisure*, that we would do much more business during the big fall buying season than we had done in January. But success in one medium during one month isn't good enough reason to expand the logic to include every other magazine in America. Each magazine seems to pose individual problems as well as individual possibilities. Take a magazine such as *Woman's Day*, which is sold in grocery stores. One would think that running $5 and $10 items would bring an enormous number of orders. But this was not the case, and, for the amount of money invested, the Kenton Collection got few orders from the *Woman's Day* ads. Maybe the fault was in the choices we offered, but, whatever it was, our use of the magazine didn't work. We discovered we needed to "profile" each publication, not lump them together as "magazines."

I think the reason I have had so much to say on the magazine advertising failure is that, frankly, it knocked me off my pedestal. I had gone into the mail-order business with a host of assumptions and assurances; assured of certain certainties, to quote T. S. Eliot. The first year's million-dollar loss was predicted, but the second year we thought we knew the ropes. The magazine experiment hurt my faith in my assumptions— which had been not guesses but careful calculations. It also injured my belief in the reliability of old friends, which may have been unrealistic on the face of it but had been part of my personal code.

Seeking the silver lining of every cloud, however, I guess that if we had not been so deeply in debt due to the ad program, the Riklis group might have considered the Collection an asset worth holding onto and I would never have been able to buy it.

Here then, are my twenty-five best mistakes, mainly in the form of "Don'ts."

- Always look for the worst possibilities first.
- Take your markdowns as soon as possible—in merchandise and in people.
- Don't deal with the same sources all the time, whether banks, printers, photographers, art directors, paper mills, box manufacturers, or designers. It makes them feel too secure, and pretty soon your business is taken for granted and someone else is treated better.
- Don't be too dependent on one source for any one project.
- Don't think declines in the economy will not affect your business. Heed the signs at the earliest moment.
- Don't experiment until you have set aside the amount of money you plan to lose. Budget in advance of the experiment, not as it is going on.
- Don't hire friends, don't buy from friends, don't borrow money from friends. (I'll confess, I still do one or another of these "Don'ts" from time to time, despite my experiences.)
- Don't worry too much about competition; mind your own business.
- Don't start with quantity, start with quality—in merchandise and in employees. Pick people you think you can spend long periods of time with.
- Don't expand for greatness until greatness comes near.
- Don't listen to outsiders who want either to do you a favor or to save you money. "Save you money" is a sure signal that you are targeted to spend money on someone else.
- Don't accept internal recommendations without making sure you understand all the internal relationships.
- Don't involve yourself, as boss, in intracompany gossip; keep aware but keep aloof.
- Don't let the Suggestion Box be just for complaints.
- Don't think your personal objectives will stay the same.

- Don't waste time with schemers—and the more serious the scheme, the more the loss.
- Don't buy something "about to be made."
- Don't send employees on buying trips until you see concrete evidence of their ideas of quality and taste.
- Don't try to outguess the credit manager; credit practices are best left to the more suspicious.
- Don't forget: Factories burn down, warehouses flood, molds break, shipments are stolen, makers break legs, and presidents die; insurmountable catastrophes are insurmountable.
- Don't believe your own press clippings.
- Don't allow success to lower your standards.
- Don't forget: more people, more problems.
- Don't assume people are honest. A security system protects the honest as much as it uncovers the dishonest.
- Don't assume people are dishonest; it destroys good working conditions.

IX

Collecting Famous Names and Infamous Lawsuits

AFTER THE SALE OF the Kenton Collection had been made, nearly six months late, we had to split the tax year with the Kenton Corporation. Ironically, it was the best "year" Kenton had, because, by the time of the closing, it could be seen that the Collection catalogue was going to be, finally, a success. We continued with the Kenton name for the remainder of 1973, as agreed in the contract of sale, but our house list had grown and we could see the true response coming from that part of our list: the 200,000 total of our buying customers, the group we *knew* would buy because we had sold to its members.

I don't know what Riklis thought during those days when he had already turned loose of the Collection and it was showing its true potential. I suppose, with his 15 percent slice of the profits, per contract, he felt it was a good deal for him. We certainly didn't unleash a lot of secret weapons we had been holding back; we simply profited from our costly lessons. Otherwise, we continued to run the Collection the same way we had run it the first two years.

What did I learn from the sale and transfer of the Collection? Well, in a broad sense, I learned one must be a lot more precise in the raising of money and financing of major projects than just having a good reputation or knowing people socially. Nobody takes your word for things when big money is involved. Of course, if I had known more about the labyrinthine ways of the financial world I probably never would have attempted to buy the Collection. I would have known that a small bank must count on a larger bank buying the overline on a loan, and I would have known that the board of directors of the smaller bank, knowing little about me, would face great problems. (In a coincidental turn of events, as years passed and my business quickly became successful, I became a stockholder and a board member of Brookhollow National, the small bank, and I learned how difficult it was to make a big loan to someone like me when the board didn't even know me, and when the members were having arguments with Jim Clark, their president, and Jim was having difficulties with the larger bank. But Jim made the deal happen, and he deserves my permanent thanks.)

So . . . I had spent one million dollars, first, for the right to run a shaky business and, second, for the use of a list of names which, by that time, we had taught ourselves to believe in.

Well, it was as if someone magically pulled the curtain and the real drama began, those months of 1973 when the Collection was finally mine. Our business turned around, and by fall we were able to predict a $5 million return from the Christmas book. One unexpected assist was the oil embargo of late 1973 and early 1974. It was so much easier to shop from a catalogue, in those first days of long lines at the gas stations. Of course, the energy crisis didn't end, and we still face fuel short-ages, but impact of the panic of 1973 and 1974 faded, even though gasoline prices never did.

An interesting customer surfaced during that time—my old boss, Stanley Marcus. He ordered a $10.50 item from the cata-logue and demanded personal delivery "to save postage." I de-livered it myself and he bought my lunch.

The catalogue settled down to a statistical mix I thought would hold forever. Our 1973 books were 95 percent gifts and housewares and only 5 percent fashions (clothing and apparel accessories). Fashion would later expand greatly, and apparel, for men and women, would fill 20 percent to half our books some years. Mail-order formulas can't become rigid.

I had been doing all the buying, with Carolyn's help, but in 1973 I hired Allen Rushing to assist. He was our Vice-Presi-dent and Senior Buyer. The very first item he bought for the Horchow catalogue was a pewter-backed military hairbrush . . . and it still runs, now with initials added—another of his ideas.

I look back over some trade-journal interviews from that pe-riod, and I'm pleased to see that, on fundamental principles, I haven't changed a whole lot. I told Hazel Mosely, of *Women's Wear Daily*, that I was intensely personal in picking catalogue items, carrying around mental "profiles" of about twenty-five people, and, if I could think of one of them who might like something, I would buy it—or, the reverse, if I couldn't I wouldn't.

I also noted that trend-setting was not a factor in our selec-tions. "I don't care if I don't have it first," I told her. I pointed out that Halston's Ultrasuede dress was (then) everywhere, but we sold six hundred of them, along with a Diane Von Fur-stenberg shirtdress and a Geoffrey Beene blouse which were best-sellers on the open market but also best-sellers for us. "If it's already run we know the kinks are out and the buttonholes are right," I said.

I still feel that way about fashion exclusives. We have a number of exclusives in our catalogue—a quite high percentage, in fact—but they are not tied into fashion or style trends very often. Our word "exclusive" indicates items we have either commissioned or developed from scratch, or, in all cases, items which will be found *only* in the Horchow catalogue. When we see that a fashion has succeeded, we offer it in as attractive a style as can be found, and in some cases we will continue to offer it after the trendy outlets may have downplayed it—but we never chase fashion trends.

This was about the time I experienced one of my most embarrassing moments. I was in London on a buying trip and was to have dinner with Bob and Grace Fowler, friends whose house I had never visited before. I had their address down as 21 Cadogan, and when I told the taxi driver "Cadogan," he asked, "Cadogan Place?" and I said, "Yes, and please hurry."

I arrived at 21 Cadogan Place and knocked. The butler opened the door, and I said I was expected for dinner. The butler made me a drink and said he would notify the host. In a moment a man appeared and I thought he must be a friend of Bob's. I introduced myself and said something offhand but friendly. The man looked quizzically at me and asked what I wanted.

I said, "I'm just waiting for Bob and Grace."

He looked pained and said, "I'm afraid there's been a mistake. This is my house and there's no 'Bob and Grace' here."

Then it dawned on me, I had wanted Cadogan Square, not Cadogan Place. Amid apologies, my involuntary host told me, "Please finish your drink," which I did. It turned out my true destination was not so far from there.

London addresses must be given very precisely.

*　*　*

By the beginning of 1974 (when we adopted the Horchow name), people like Princess Grace of Monaco (she bought lucite bathroom accessories), some Rothschilds, du Ponts, Kennedys, and Rockefellers had become steady customers, along with a couple of dozen movie and television stars. But the rent payers were ten customers who were spending over $10,000 a year with us. I must admit, I hadn't thought there would be that many people who would spend that much on a regular basis with a mail-order firm unless the firm was in the business of selling yachts or diamonds. Another thing I learned was to make it as easy as possible to order. I once made the statement that we took pains to make the order blank simple enough "for Mrs. Taylor in Amarillo who hates to fill out forms." Several Mrs. Taylors, from all over the nation, complained I made them sound lazy or stupid, so I dropped the name—although there really is a Mrs. Taylor from Amarillo who had said she hated to fill out forms and asked us, please, not to make ours tedious.

When ordering from us, we have never required our customers to do any more work than they want to do. We were happy to fill orders for a Chicago customer who simply yanked pages out of the catalogues, circled the items she wanted, and marked "2," "5," or (in her case) "10" across the picture. Some years her orders, done that way, amounted to $50,000, and, once we knew that when she wrote "5" or "10" she meant exactly that, we disregarded the lack of proper forms.

Let me jump ahead of my chronology a few years and tell about another amusing, and lucrative, episode involving order blanks that occurred in 1978.

Early that summer we received a rather poorly written letter from Kuwait, on plain paper, printed in all capitals. "I heard you have a luxury catalogue," the letter stated. "I have many friends who like to buy luxury. If you send me the catalogue we might buy something."

I had two or three catalogues sent and thought little more about it, because by 1978 we were getting orders from every corner of the world and foreign letters were no novelty. Shortly, we got a group of orders from Kuwait amounting to $3,000 or $4,000. Jim May and Carmen Aguirre of the order department rushed into my office with the order, but I didn't connect any of it with the letter I had received. Then another letter came, similar to the first, which read, "I appreciate the merchandise you sent. It looks very nice. Everybody liked it. But why did you not send us any more order blanks? How can we buy anything more? There is so much we want more, but you did not send any more order blanks."

I told Jim to ship the man a stack of catalogues, each containing a single order blank. (The order blanks are bound in at the printer's so we don't ordinarily keep lots of order blanks by themselves on hand.) We got back an order for nearly $20,000 worth of merchandise, accompanied by a third letter which sounded somewhat hurt: "Unless you send us more order blanks we are not going to buy any more from you."

I told Jim, "Go rip fifty order blanks out of the catalogues and send them air mail . . . we've set up a whole antagonistic relationship because we're not pushing fast enough. Have you ever known this to happen before?" Jim agreed it was a unique situation.

I wrote to the young man (we now assumed he was young) explaining that sufficient order blanks were on the way, but also assuring him he didn't need an order blank, he could just write a description of whatever he wanted on a sheet of paper, or tear out the page and use it.

The young man wrote back delighted, "We loved everything. I want five of everything in your catalogue because I know my friends want it." That order was shipped, and back came another letter. "Why don't you let me be your agent?" it asked. "I have nothing to do because my father and my family are so much in oil business and I don't like that business, but I like your catalogue, so I want to be your agent."

You may be sure I was interested—although the Horchow organization has no sales agents. I wrote and asked, "What does it mean, being my agent?"

He replied, "It means, every time you send out a catalogue you will send me ten copies and two hundred order blanks and I will see that the orders come to you, and then I will be your agent."

He didn't want money, he just wanted to be my "agent" and be involved in this pretty commercial world. And so, all of a sudden, from one little letter, I had a ready-made market which has, to date, ordered as many as one hundred of an item. And I have tried, from time to time, to include some gift or special favor for the young man who began it all—but all he seems to really want is that designation, "agent," which is quite all right with me.

As word spread through the trade in 1973 that we were now independent of the Kenton Corporation, we began to get increased attention from name designers as well as small craftmakers. They not only beat a path to our Dallas door to offer wares, but friends and business associates offered suggestions about things they had seen or knew about which they felt would fit the catalogue requirements. Geoffrey Beene, for instance, told me about an arresting kind of French vinegar that found its way into the book. My mother and my mother-in-law have always been full of "finds," several of which have worked quite well. Even my oldest daughter, Regen, once alerted me to a type of Mexican bandana of which we sold over five thousand dozen. As I wrote earlier, we have always tried to use as many handmade items as possible. In 1973 we featured some eyelet pillows done by a Dallas woman along with a Fort Worth artist's needlework, but, even that early, the problem of reorders was becoming staggering. And when you gamble on something—as I once did on a unique little pot of herbs—thinking you have your supply problem licked, you can't always anticipate international politics. The pottery that made the ceramic pots ran out of fuel for its furnaces during the oil embargo.

International politics played into our hands on another occasion. When President Nixon first got the People's Republic of China open, we had already bought some hand-painted Chinese eggs, on stands, by way of an Italian supplier. The duty was horrible (100 percent), so we had cautiously bought only a thousand. Our catalogue came out exactly when the Chinese visits and cultural exchange took place. We had a Chinese page and scooped everybody. We also got orders for ten thousand of the eggs. We tried other importers, but the eggs had turned out to be a commercial nightmare because they were so easily broken. The eggs suffered but our reputation soared.

Sometimes price is no object, literally. Once Carolyn found a beautiful little porcelain pansy ring like one her mother had had when Carolyn was a girl. It was made in Italy and we planned to offer it for $10. But, somehow, the pansy ring got into the catalogue with no copy and no price. Just the picture of it. Despite that, it sold $8,000 worth, and a lot of people who ordered one said they didn't even know what it was, they just liked the picture. (We ran the pansy ring again in 1979—with copy and price this time. Although it sold well, would you believe it actually did better before, with no description and no price?)

Then there were my precious Himalayan antique chests, which went on sale at $1,750 and sold zero, then were reduced to $995 and still didn't sell (I bought one for myself). I still can't figure it out. "Hope springs eternal" is what Allen Rushing said sarcastically, every time something like a Himalayan chest came up. I'll never admit it was a bad item; it's too beautiful, even if the chest is awkward, dark, slanted, tilted, rough-hewn, huge, and mysterious. I have gone through the list of possible reasons for the lack of sales: Was the picture unappealing, the copy unclear, the season wrong? I still have no answer.

As is true with every business, we have run into legal difficulties from utterly unexpected sources. We've learned lots of lessons, few of them pleasant, but we still don't know how to anticipate those kinds of complaints. For example, our men's clothes line is named Chas. Pfeifer, which is actually a name from my wife's family. But we got a call immediately after we included the Chas. Pfeifer name in the catalogue—another Chas. Pfeifer didn't want us using our Pfeifer's name.

In the old days, when we were the Kenton Collection and the Kenton Corporation was very visible, every time people could think of anything to sue us for, they would. The same thing still happens. In one case, with Kenton, we were carrying a Christmas card from Cartier (a Kenton Corporation company), and I asked Cartier to give me a card to photograph. They gave me one that had a customer's name on it, but I was smart enough to know it's not advisable to photograph a customer's name like that, so we took some correction fluid and altered it into the name of an aunt of mine.

A letter came from a lawyer saying, "You've used my mother's name," and we wrote back saying, "No, we used my aunt's name." But we had two or three of that sort of case that we ended up paying, even though we felt they were highway robbery. When I took over and started making the decisions, I thought we would never have to face such a situation. But the years have gone on, and now Horchow is a visible company itself.

The most ridiculous minor instance involved a little embosser to stamp names and addresses on the backs of envelopes. We have offered it with names in block letters, or the customer can send in his signature and a plate will be created using that. When we were getting ready to photograph the embosser the first time, we contacted the maker and asked him to send us samples. We got the block-letter embosser with my name on it (playing it safe, I often use my name, or the name of an employee or friend on much of the merchandise), but we didn't have time to send an autograph and have a signature plate made, so the engraver sent us something and we photographed it—there was no identification except the name Polly somebody.

Next thing we knew, a letter arrived: "Dear Sir, you have used my client's name in your advertising and you've done her irreparable damage. . . ." What kind of damage did we do? You had to take a magnifying glass to tell what the signature was, and it didn't give an address or say who or where the person was. We tried to get the manufacturer to back us up, but he ducked out. We sued him, but were unable to collect . . . and we wound up paying the woman a couple of thousand dollars—all because that manufacturer sent along a signature that just happened to be around his shop.

Sometimes we feel that threats are ridiculous. In one catalogue we had a little ring with a teddy bear attached to it, and the first mail that came after we had sent out the catalogue included a letter which said, in effect, "We are the lawyers for the Franklin Mint and the Franklin Mint owns the word 'Teddy Bear' for jewelry and you have no right to use it. Stop right now."

That one was answered with a question: "Since when is 'Teddy Bear' a privately owned word? If nothing else, it's been in use since President Theodore Roosevelt's day and is long since in public domain."

In one of our Christmas 1978 catalogues we offered a

charming collection of circus animals, performers, and accessories from Germany (toy figures, I hasten to explain), and used a line reading, "the greatest little show on earth." Shortly after that we got a very stern, threatening letter from Ringling Brothers, Barnum & Bailey's lawyers demanding all sorts of things because, according to them, we had violated their trademark, "The Greatest Show on Earth." We disregarded the threats, but I instructed my copywriters to stop giving Ringling Brothers, Barnum & Bailey free publicity, if they felt that way.

Several corporations do this, many of them taking things to ridiculous lengths, claiming they must protect their trademark name or it will pass into public domain and become part of everyday language. It has always seemed to me that this would be desirable—for everyone to refer to any soft drink as "Coke®" or every camera as "Kodak.®" I wish everyone in America would refer to every mail-order catalogue as "Horchow."

I wish all these trademark violation stories were as amusing and simple as the ones I've mentioned, but, on a few occasions, we have been bulldozed, more or less, by someone so much bigger than we are that we simply couldn't afford to stand up to them, even though we might eventually have proved our side right.

Once, a few years back, I received a letter from a man who sold me luggage and he said that he was contacted by Halston to do a luggage promotion. He noticed that the fabric was quite similar to ours in that it was imprinted with an "H" design and he just wondered if it was all right.

I wrote back and said not only was it *not* all right, but Halston was using *our* H's. About the same time this was going on, Fieldcrest sheets and towels came out with the interlocking H's—for Halston. It made me mad, so I took it to my lawyer and asked, "Don't we have the trademark on this?" He said we did, and he wrote a letter to Halston to cease and desist. Well, barely a week had gone by when the Halston people served us with a suit. They alleged we were stealing *their* trademark! They showed all the different forms of H's they had registered, and it turned out we had only registered those interlocking H's going 2-3-2 with a square around them formed by the words "Horchow Collection." But Halston had registered the H's sort of free-floating and adjoining, and the only way we owned them was stacked 2-3-2. Norton Simon, who owns Halston, is a whole lot bigger than Horchow, so, after things had gone on and on, we finally had to agree to their use of the H's, and we were allowed to use our H's on anything that we currently had but couldn't add anything to them.

And so, after many thousands of dollars of wasted lawyers' fees on our part, we were "allowed" to use our own trademark. I hear more and more people say, "Who wants to have someone else's initials all over things?" But, at the time we did it, the consumers seemed to want it.

As I said, we get into fights with the biggest. Take Exxon as another example. There was a designer and fabricator I had known around the industry for years, who had a cute idea (I thought). It was a sort of Christmas card, on plastic, with XXMAS GREETINGS arranged across the top, with a blank space for your name. It looked like a credit card.

I liked the card idea, but I saw that it looked vaguely like an Exxon credit card, so I asked the designer, "Are you sure this is all right?"

He was quite positive. "Of course. . . . It doesn't say 'Exxon' it says 'Xxmas.' "

I asked several times if he was *sure* it was all right, and he repeatedly said yes. After some wrangling about which of us should have the cards manufactured, he had it made, and we put the item in our Christmas preview (August) catalogue, and immediately began receiving orders by the thousands.

But, among all those orders, we also got a registered letter from Exxon's lawyers asking us to stop selling the card that minute. Not only did we have to stop production and sales, we had to destroy all the cards we had, and then we had to write a letter to everyone who ordered the cards, and, if we didn't do that, we had to write everyone who got a catalogue (two million people) and tell them we didn't have any right to use "their trademark."

Our lawyers looked at things and said that if we went to the ultimate end of the rainbow, we had a very strong case. In the first place, the Horchow purchase order makes it plain that if a manufacturer sells me something he indemnifies me against such problems. Unfortunately, the person who sold me the cards didn't appear to have much in the way of money to lose, so it was useless to try to make him take the blame, or even share it. Exxon was coming to me because I was the one who advertised the cards. My lawyer said (again) we were in the right, that Exxon didn't own "XXMAS," and, if we wanted to spend many, many thousands on legal fees, we would eventually win, but it could go on forever, and Exxon was, after all, the first or second or third largest corporation in the world . . . and did we really want to play David and Goliath?

I really did, it made me so damn mad to have to be pushed around by a huge corporation just because we couldn't afford to spend the money to battle with them, but then I decided it was just frittering away money (there was no way we could have ever recouped it through sale of the Christmas cards), so I accepted Exxon's terms.

It is one of the injustices of the world that a giant can just say, "You can't do that," or, "You must do this," and you have to cooperate. And what made it even worse was, they made us send a letter to everyone who ordered those cards, a letter written by them in their legal terms, with a flip reference to the tigers in their tanks and a statement that they were not in the mail-order business. I would have fired anyone in our advertising and promotion department who sent out a letter like that under our name. It really wasn't our style at all.

Fortunately, at the point at which we got the legal ukase, none of the Xxmas cards had been delivered by my unreliable supplier, so we had never actually mailed any cards. When we got the cards, however, we had to mail them to New York for Exxon to destroy. So we paid for the cards, paid for the freight, paid for the letters—and they destroyed them and we lost $35,000 worth of sales. (To add insult to injury, we had to pay the man who had caused all the trouble by assuring me the cards were all right.)

All this cost and embarrassment was over something that Exxon controlled by its sheer size, not by right or by law. It was entirely a case of size. It made all of us really mad, and we had a little ceremony at which we formally chopped up our Exxon credit cards (the real Exxon credit cards) and bad-mouthed the Goliath in our little way.

Well, that wasn't the end of the Exxon Xxmas story, as it turned out. A customer who had ordered the Christmas cards wrote me, furious, and said she had sent a copy of her letter to everybody from Ralph Nader, the Attorney General, and Ted Kennedy to the Chairman of the Board of Exxon. About two weeks after this, Jack Anderson, the newspaper columnist, called and asked what it was all about. We told him, and in a few days Jack Anderson wrote that here we were, the Horchow mail-order firm down in Texas, being slapped around by Exxon the giant, just because Exxon had the muscle to do it. We got more publicity than we could ever have paid for. I received dozens of carbons of letters of protest sent to the Exxon administrators, and to high government officials . . . but as far as I know it never stirred Goliath a bit. However, getting a sympathetic story in nine hundred papers may have been worth the $35,000 we lost on the card sales, so, out of a bad situation can come some good . . . sometimes.

I am not sure which is more frightening, to be muscled by an unjust Goliath or to be the victim of dull-minded bureaucracy. The first Christmas catalogue we put together had the photograph in it of a wallet with real money. I remembered from Neiman–Marcus days the restrictions on photographing U.S. currency: You couldn't photograph it in color or photograph the entire bill, and you either had to reduce the bill to half- or quarter-size or enlarge it to significant increases. We did everything correctly.

However, someone called the Federal Bureau of Investigation and they sicked the Treasury Department on us. I'm not sure what the informant said, or what the FBI told the Treasury agents, but I do not believe anyone looked at our catalogue. They accepted someone's hint that we had illegally photographed U.S. currency. (In fact, I'm not sure the government bureaucrats even knew how the law read on the matter.)

Whatever the case, one morning those agents came stomping into my office (this was in the Nixon days) and began acting as if they were raiding a counterfeit ring. It was very scary. One of them said to me, "We are here to confiscate all of your catalogues," as if I kept them hidden in my coat closet—all one million or so of them. It was like an invasion of storm troopers.

I finally got them to tell me what we had supposedly done wrong. When I found out, I quickly called the lawyers and the lawyers said we were absolutely all right, that we had followed federal regulations to the letter—in fact, had shown only the corners of some bills sticking out of the wallet. I told my lawyer, on the phone, "You can't convince these guys. They want to confiscate the catalogues."

Fortunately, most of the catalogues had been mailed and we

had maybe twenty or thirty around the office. In the presence of the Treasury agents, we had to take those few catalogues and tear out those pages. I truly believe that if the agents had thought we would do it, they would have required we call every customer and demand the catalogue back.

That episode was really frightening, and it was wrong. We hadn't done anything against the law, but, by the time we proved it, we could have been out of business, or in terrible trouble. It was a very unjust thing.

When I finally got a little friendlier with the agents, after about two weeks, I asked one of them, "What caused all this? Who told you we were violating the law?"

"It was reported to us," he said, not at all happy at my questioning.

I insisted, "Who reported it?"

And he shook his head, "I can't tell you." Then he grinned a little and said, "Someone that doesn't care much about you." I'm pretty sure I know who it was.

It may have been done more or less as a joke to begin with, although I doubt it, but what might have been started as a joke wasn't taken humorously by the Treasury Department—or by me.

But you can't presume anything is safe, or that anyone with "celebrity" status will be understanding because of past favors. In one of our catalogues we pictured a portable black-and-white television set. I had told the photographers I wanted an actual transmission on the screen, not a simulated reception. When they turned on the set to take a picture of it an old movie was on, so a picture of an actor appeared on the portable set's screen . . . or it was *supposed* to be an actor; it looked like some television newscaster to me. The picture printed in the catalogue is, literally, about the size of a man's thumbnail. But, the next thing I knew, I got a letter from a lawyer in Beverly Hills saying, "You have used my client's picture without his permission. We're suing for damages."

For a while I tried to convince myself that the actor didn't know about his lawyer's threat. Friends of mine and his wrote him, attempting to remind him that the Horchow organization had been friendly: We had once sent, at his agent's request, several hundred dollars worth of camping goods and clothing without charge to a Canadian location where he was shooting a picture. But no reply was ever made to the friends' letters.

A couple of months after I had heard from the lawyer, a friend called and said her mother, in California, had sent her a clipping from a local newspaper which told of a $150,000 suit being filed against Horchow by the actor, alleging we had damaged his earning ability to do commercials. It was the first I had heard about it. I found it hard to believe, but there it was, and it eventually was carried in hundreds of newspapers nationally, so I guess (putting the best face on it possible) we got a bit of publicity from it—not that it was worth the cost.

I don't have room in one book to list all the amused comments that have been made about "a name like Horchow" being used for a business, but I fully expect another Roger Horchow to appear out of the woodwork someday and claim he has been damaged somehow.

X

Horchow? Will It Play the U.S. Mails?

ON JANUARY 1, 1974, AS we had agreed in the sale contract, we changed our name from Kenton Collection to Horchow Collection. I was determined to stamp "Horchow" on everything, including the minds of our customers. Some of my Dallas friends joked about my using the name so much during the first Horchow Collection catalogues, asking if I didn't think I was taking S. Roger Horchow too seriously, sticking his initials on all the monogrammed pieces and scratching his business and social notes in all the diaries and appointment calendars.

We were very worried that our business would fall apart. I accepted the fact that "Horchow" isn't very commercial-sounding (it does beat "Horchowsky," the European family name), but I wanted it to stand for something, to be identified with pleasant expectations in the minds of our readers. I wasn't on an ego trip. After all, who knew Aaron Montgomery Ward in 1872, when he more or less invented American mail-order shopping?

I felt, and Carolyn and the board felt, that we needed to hire someone in public relations to help us make the change from Kenton to something else (Horchow was not the only name we considered). Through a friend of mine, Phyllis Flood, I met Tish Baldrige and hired her to help change our name and get through our transition period. As it turned out, we really didn't need the help in the beginning because the first time we mailed a Horchow catalogue—merely inserting the name "Horchow" where "Kenton" had been—we were off and running; the name change proved never to be a factor. But Tish's ideas were so helpful, and we became such good friends, that after that she stayed on retainer, helping us with various projects.

Our catalogues are still full of personal references, although the general reader doesn't know that some of the little notes are about family affairs. We now send too many books to use my girls as models more than once a year, although they are all three of professional model capability—I say this as a catalogue publisher, not just a fond father. Regen is a dark beauty, willowy like her mother. Elizabeth (Lizzie) is rather tall and slender, with a pretty, open look about her. Sally, still a youngster as this is written, is a cut-up, full of jokes and laughter, with a wise little face. Using the names of friends is not only convenient but useful. If we tried to make up as many names as we need in the catalogue, it wouldn't be long until people would be writing and calling by the hundreds, as I explained in a previous chapter.

A great many of the little scribbles in the Horchow catalogues are inside jokes, as many of you have probably observed. I sometimes included the names of my favorites, Dorothy and the late Richard Rodgers, to honor them or say hello in the catalogue notes. We also have an "Ernest Fitzgerald" and a

"Zelda Hemingway" listed as guests in an open hostess book, although the real people, Ernest Hemingway and Zelda Fitzgerald, were reported to have hated each other intensely. Most of the names used on signs or personalized items are from our board of directors or involve things they own or have done. We offered a line of leather-bound blank books with humorous titles to be selected with someone's name added as author, and we used my secretary's name (*Yet Unpublished Poems* by Pat Puddington) and my name (*Acceptable Excuses* by S. Roger Horchow) as examples. The idea went over very well, but I would blush to print what some customers wanted on books, especially titles attributed to certain politicians. We had to reject a few we were asked to print on the books, motivated about as much by decency as by fear of libel. We tried to be broadminded, but finally appointed our Customer Service director Kitty Lane to pass on the more outré and risqué suggestions.

At about that same time we offered to make a blown-up jigsaw puzzle from any photograph sent us, and, again, Kitty Lane had to be called in to decide. Some of the snapshots that were sent were hard to believe. We reached the point where mere nudity—front, side, or back—was routine, although the majority were photos of family, friends, or beloved scenes.

I must also add this anecdote: One catalogue reader took Pat Puddington's blank book title to heart and wrote offering consolations, saying that he, too, had a book full of "yet unpublished poems" and for her not to give up. I think it inspired her to become a poet.

A few years ago a customer wrote and suggested we ought to be doing business with Fleur Cowles (Meyer), the innovative American artist who, in the 1950s, created that brief-lived but dazzling magazine, *Flair*. I went to see her in London and was quite impressed with her art, especially a series of lithographs which she said she had done with no commercial intentions. I asked if I could offer them in a limited edition, and she agreed. She had just been made a member of the board of the World Wildlife Fund, and her interest in the organization aroused my own, so I decided to give a share of our profits from the sale of the lithographs to the Fund. The first of the series of five editions was offered for $140 or $160, with an option to buy the next four. It was purely an experiment, and I don't think Fleur or I ever dreamed the offering would be a sellout, at $700 the set. In two weeks the entire series was completely gone.

I was delighted, because I thought this might open a whole new area of fine art by mail. So, a few months later, we devoted an entire catalogue to art: all media, all prices, mainly modern—and it flopped. That took me back to my earlier contention, that the mail-order business is primarily one of items, not lines. In contrast to the catalogue-full of art, Fleur Cowles's lithographs, while fairly costly, were an item, something buyers wanted just for themselves. (On top of that, we hadn't researched our market well enough to pinpoint which of our customers were most interested in art.)

With this same concept, we tried a catalogue devoted solely to office items. It did better than the art book, but not sufficiently better to cause it to exceed what we might have done offering the same material in various Horchow catalogues. We tried a kitchen issue and it had similar results. Maybe if we had tried to establish a line of kitchen-inspired things it would have worked after enough mailings (there are now a couple such catalogues) but why go to the trouble when the same, or better, results can be had with your established product?

Fleur Cowles was helpful to the Collection. She told us about some hand embroidery done by nuns in a small Spanish town. She was anxious to help these nuns, so she designed a beautiful holly motif, which the nuns embroidered for us on linen napkins. They were offered in the catalogue at $100 per dozen, and were a great Christmas success. She also did other lithographs, and a version of "The Peaceable Kingdom" for needlepoint. Fifteen percent of the proceeds from this sale was given to the World Wildlife Fund, too. We have continued the donation process whenever we can, and, through the years, the Horchow Collection has contributed a percentage of sales to causes ranging from Children's Television Workshop, the World Wildlife Fund, and the American Heart Association, to the American Institute for Public Service, "Sesame Street," and the Dallas Museum of Fine Arts. I have been a vice-president of the World Wildlife Fund Corporate Fund Drive, which raises money to protect and replenish endangered species of both animals and plants around the world. The Horchow organization has been able to contribute several thousand dollars, I'm proud to say, and Fleur Cowles's artistic offerings continue in our catalogues. Her greatest contribution to our work, personally, was to get me interested in the Fund's cause.

The Horchow Collection was so successful that first year of separate ownership that I was able to pay off our bank loans almost immediately, then set about buying out the investors who had bought our stock and debenture packages. To do this I paid five-to-one on the original investment. We were also successful in our professional way. We were awarded the Silver Mailbox by the Direct Mail Marketing Association, which is the industry's Oscar for best mail-order catalogue. Three very big companies tried to buy us during 1974, at a staggering profit to us, so I knew we had arrived nationally.

But we were still making mistakes. Early in the year we issued a British catalogue, translating the prices to English money, and we planned to issue French and West German catalogues if the British book succeeded. But sales failed to reach our ambitious expectations, and we gave up on European expansion. We also organized a wholesale division called "The Collection" through a gift wholesaler, but that didn't last long.

A much more serious mistake was our alternative catalogue which we issued under the name "Weston Trading Co., Ltd." (There was no special reason for the name. It just had a straightforward sound.) This mistake began in a quite valid way. I had read in *Business Week* about a Harvard Business School management course which one could only attend if one's business did under a certain amount per year and if one were the chief executive officer. This was a nine-week course which could be taken over a longer period by going three weeks at a time. While I thought I knew merchandising and buying, I didn't know enough about business itself. I signed up for the first of the three units, but it wasn't as valuable as I had hoped. I was the only one enrolled who was in my kind of business. I did learn to read a balance sheet, which is very important, and which plenty of executives can't do.

The class did case studies of various business triumphs and failures. One case was the Brown Shoe Company, an actual firm. The idea we got from the Brown Shoe Company case was that in times when things got bad you offered different layers of business, including something for the lowest, but, if things got really good, you also had a line to push with the rich. I interpolated the Brown Shoe Company case into our business and decided Horchow should have another company with different taste levels and lower prices to protect us if a recession came (this was about the time of the original oil embargo) or, in any case, just to compete with ourselves.

The idea wasn't a bad one, but we went at it wrong. For one thing, we had operated under the assumption that 70 percent of our customers lived in that narrow Eastern seaboard corridor from Maine to Richmond. We figured a big savings on freight and other shipping costs if we had a facility central to that area, so we opened a 73,000-square-foot warehouse on Long Island to handle both Horchow orders and those of the new Weston Trading Co. Secondly, our theory was that we only got ten orders out of every one hundred Horchow catalogues mailed, so there were ninety people out there receiving our book and not buying. Why not tap them with another, different book? Also, I felt there must be a segment of potential customers who were a bit inhibited by luxury catalogues. They might have the same income as a Horchow customer but not the same taste.

Actually, these thoughts weren't far off the mark, but, as I said, I approached it in the wrong way. I had my associate from Jensen days, Tom Wendorff, pick the Weston merchandise, keeping it middle-of-the-road. The new catalogue was launched in time for Christmas, and the customers liked it, but they didn't like it enough. Then the merchandise began overlapping with Horchow, and by spring the subsidiary company was showing losses because it was saddled with the Long Island facility; this expansion was proving to be a costly mistake. Also, to mail one Weston Trading Co. catalogue cost the same as a Horchow catalogue, and the Horchow book did twice as much business. We discontinued Weston and pulled out of Long Island, back to the one facility at Dallas.

But the Weston Trading Co., Ltd. wasn't my worst mistake during that period. That experience was still to come.

XI

Some People (Me) Never Learn

I SUPPOSE I SHOULD title this section, "Never Do Business With Friends: Part II." During the time of rapid expansion, when Horchow was becoming its own entity, it was considered by my board to be a matter of great urgency that some sort of orderly management succession be developed. The idea was that I find someone who could take over the day-to-day operation and supervise the various sections so I could spend my time with merchandising and catalogue preparation. It seemed like a fairly straightforward job, requiring skills of management rather than any specific mail-order talents.

As I mentioned before, I have always kept in touch with old friends. During this time when we were searching for a general manager, an old Army friend happened to pass through Dallas and stopped to have dinner. He and I had been in the Army Security Agency in 1952, sitting side by side for over a year. He stayed in the Army, and we exchanged letters from time to time. By the time he came through Dallas, he had become a full colonel with all the credentials of a career officer. His ability at his work had been superior, and he had commanded thousands of men, taken care of large dollar-volume budgets, and met many important deadlines. It struck me, when he arrived, that here was the perfect candidate for our general-manager position. As we finished our dinner I decided I should talk him into leaving the Army (which he had hinted at doing anyway), and joining us.

He did retire and moved to Dallas to start helping run the company. His short-term goal was to learn everything he could about the firm, its people, and its procedures. Then, as each task became fully understood, it would be assigned either to him or to someone he designated, so that we would have a clear delegation of responsibility. As his first year with us went on, it was a real pleasure to have someone who would take over so much of the work from me, and who seemed to enjoy it so much.

There was never a task or assignment which Colonel D. turned down, and he gradually took over many of the activities I formerly controlled. This was during a time when I was busy expanding my own spheres of influence, examining the whole concept of the company, and absorbing the growing evidence that we were going to succeed. After losing so long, we had embarked on a time of great profits, with sales exceeding $9 million and a pre-tax gain of nearly a million. All was well, and no one could do much wrong.

I've learned, upon reflection, that good times can be very dangerous, because in good times one tends to overlook all the danger signals. People began to comment that Colonel D. was running our company just like the Army. All of a sudden, we had a superstructure of people funneling reports to one head, namely him. When I noticed I was getting very little information about the operation, I should have immediately taken stock of where things stood. Instead, I acted on the assumption that with a million in profits and $9 million in sales, we had to be doing a great deal right, and I had no cause to worry.

But a serious situation developed. As time went along the company became polarized, and the Colonel and I were on a collision course. I was working to sign up what I thought were bright young people, and, at the same moment, he had recruited what I felt to be Army types who were used to his highly structured, more rigid ways. Soon we had a reporting system which kept me more or less in the dark. By the spring of 1975, so much trust had been given away on my part, that events occurred within the company without my even getting a chance to find out what was happening. It was absolutely my own fault, and it taught me another good lesson: No matter how much trust you have in your associates, you must check very thoroughly to be sure that you know all that goes on all the time.

When you have an Army-type management, everyone seems to hide everything from the next person along the chain in an effort to protect his or her job. This is often said of government and Civil Service, but it applies to a small business as well. At all costs, the theory goes, you must keep bad news from the next person up. Being at the top of the pyramid, I felt I was always the last one to hear the bad news. Fortunately for me, I am nosy and curious enough so that I can't sit isolated in my office, waiting to be told everything. Despite some polarization within my own firm, I eventually had enough information filtering in to realize I had better regain control. I thought it was doubly difficult for me to discover facts, because by then there were opposing camps in the organization, and the tendency is always to believe one camp is 100 percent right and the other camp is 100 percent wrong—which, of course, is never 100 percent true. During that difficult spring of 1975, it was almost impossible to separate fact, hate, and rumor-mongering.

Earlier that year we had bought out our investors, taking over a million dollars out of the company to do so. We had thought we would have the money available as surplus, only to find that, instead of the surplus cash, we had a million dollars of inventory that had to be disposed of—and that was the straw that broke the camel's back. To pay off the investors, I had to negotiate a very large line of credit at the bank, against which we drew immediately. We finally determined we must have a true housecleaning: a gigantic garage sale.

Where we had occasionally sold our excess merchandise in the warehouse with a weekend sale of half-price goods, this time we went out and rented a very large market hall in Dallas and planned a full week's extravaganza—which, as it turned out, would be the final battle by our "Army" group. It was organized as lavishly as a small version of the Normandy invasion.

I thought the extra planning was money in the bank. As I later learned, our employees were keyed up and worked hard because they had been told the merchandise they carried to the sale site would never have to reenter the warehouse; it was "good-bye!" With this incentive, everyone was superactive in cleaning out merchandise, and some of it, we learned too late, was unnecessary zeal. I was to recall, many times, my own brash "clean-up" of old stock at Neiman–Marcus when I first went to work there.

Now let me explain that all this "wisdom" I have been mentioning comes from hindsight. At the time I still had much faith in the ability of the military to carry off the great Dallas Garage Sale. I even left town to go to a Hill School class reunion, and, when I returned, I learned, looking at the full-page news picture of the crowd that we had supposedly carried out "the outstanding marketing event of Dallas, comparable only to the Neiman–Marcus Fortnight." It was an outstanding marketing event, all right, and though it brought us half a million dollars in cash, it didn't bring the needed million—and we ended up losing an additional $150,000 not so much from price reductions as from what I felt were mistakes of logistics made during the time of the great "battle."

One of the unusual twists to the Garage Sale was the use of an auctioneer, who would take large lots of merchandise and knock them down to dealers, who had been notified to come to the last day of the sale. This might have been a fairly good way to handle the leftovers (if they had needed handling in the first place), but we didn't prepare for the facts of life of an auction—another case of business naiveté. The auctioneer had been given no base price to start bids with, and we had no one in the audience to pick up the low bids; consequently, we simply gave away merchandise for around two cents on the retail dollar instead of achieving something like break-even.

Then, all the bills started coming in. Colonel D.'s aide-de-camp had arranged with the food purveyor to provide Cokes and "all-you-can-eat" all day, every day, for the employees who were already getting, in many cases, overtime or double-time pay—and, on the theory of keeping the bad news from the next person up the ladder, no particular budget had been made to cover any of this. Each person involved said, after the fact, that the other one had fully understood the costs.

After steadfastly refusing to dirty my fingers by going to the sale, I learned of the promise not to return any overstock, and that that particular promise was fulfilled by Colonel D. going from table to table, slashing prices to such levels that the merchandise disappeared by magic. With the auctioneer giving it away on one side and my "Army" on the other, we, at least, cleaned house. It would have been better, of course, to have had a charitable institution come in and just haul it away, saving us time, work, and tax deductions.

Shortly after the Garage Sale we entered into an agreement to handle orders and shipping for another group of friends who wanted to produce a sports catalogue and pay us on a fee basis. As their book would not be competitive with ours, and as the other company was composed of friends, I was not opposed to the idea.

The contract, as I understood it, provided that half of the profits came to us and none of the losses. I really didn't see why the other company would be willing to do that, but I was assured by Colonel D., who had received the original proposition, that the group fully understood that the risks were all theirs, and that we were simply to provide them with the production of their catalogue, the mailing of that catalogue to our list, and the handling of their orders.

I was away on vacation and transacted my questioning by telephone, asking over and over about specific terms. Colonel D. pointed to the general Letter of Intent which did not mention making us share half the losses. I suggested we at least ask the pointed question even though we thought we knew the answer. I used to get very annoyed with Edward Marcus, when I worked for him, because, when I brought what I thought was a wonderful idea to him, he would ask so many questions, all relating to the downside possibilities, making the idea sound dangerous. To me it was a completely negative approach to business. Looking back, Mr. Marcus was absolutely right and I was absolutely wrong. One must ask the bad questions and at least be certain that the other person, or persons, are alert to the possibility that something could go wrong, and that they have some plan in mind in that case.

The contract with my friends' company was signed when I returned from vacation. The final terms gave them 100 percent of the profits and 100 percent of the losses, and simply gave us a fixed commission for handling their orders rather than a split of the profits. It seemed like a straightforward agreement, and I thought it was better for us. But, even with the careful work of their lawyers and ours, we were presently in a dispute with my friends. Everything had been set up to take care of the money that would be made, but somehow the thought that nobody would make any money hadn't occurred. The other people began questioning our methods, our book-keeping, our business procedures—everything we did that should have been understood. Within a few weeks I found myself being criticized for ruining a mail-order catalogue—and blamed for their losses.

They, in the meantime, learned lots of our hard-earned tricks of the trade, they hired one of my key employees away (plus two subsupervisors), they incurred the enmity of most of our Board of Directors (who had not been their friends, there-fore were not in a forgiving mood), and proved once and for all that you shouldn't do business with friends.

From the very first, I was just trying to be accommodating. From my point of view, that cynical motto, "No good deed goes unpunished," may not get chiseled in marble, but it's at least worthy of a fancy gold frame.

The time came, of course, when Colonel D. resigned. I felt the company was about to either slide or split from my control. But, more important, many of the workers were up in arms. As soon as word got around that I was concerned with the way the Horchow Collection had taken on some of the bureaucratic at-tributes of the U.S. Army, they came pouring into my office, each with his or her personal "horror" story about the way things were being done. It was at this point that I realized I would have to go back into the company and take complete charge if it was to survive.

All this seems, I know, to be a blanket condemnation of a dedicated man, and I don't really want it to be that. I made the first mistake when I hired someone out of friendship. You must never attribute abilities to someone hired in an advanced capacity unless those abilities are fully tested. I remembered him as having certain capabilities, but these were not the ones needed in our job. Also, it is very difficult, I am convinced, for someone to come straight from a military situation, even if that person was in command (I should say, *especially* if that person was in command) and take over a fast-moving, fast-growing company such as ours. In the military, and in some old, established firms, you have a recognized chain of command, a table of organization that designates duties and responsibilities, and you have a way of doing everything by the book so that even if you are defeated, there's a good book excuse for it—and there is a book procedure for retreating from a loss.

It was difficult to play by these rules, or even the so-called business-school rules, in our organization, and (as I had seen) we suffered when we tried it. In the mail-order business, at the level we were doing it, there was no book. We were writing the book-to-be. Some of the old basics work, but mostly they don't. When you put a rigid person with a rigid training into this undefined formula, you can almost surely predict failure of one element or another.

I know that the departure of Colonel D. was the final event in my maturity as an executive, leader, owner, or whatever term should be applied. From that day on, I have known what Roger Horchow should be doing. Notice I said *should* be doing, because I am still relearning lessons of business and life. But now I feel adequate to learn whatever lessons I have to learn, and I know there isn't some part missing that someone else has to supply. I am adequate myself—and that is as good a definition of maturity as I can think of.

XII

Copying Isn't a Threat, It's Flattery!

By MID-1975 OUR SALES were at the point, and our operation had reached the place, where we could experiment with our catalogues—indulge ourselves, so to speak. The company was now owned or controlled by Texans (my in-laws were from Arkansas, but they learned to be very understanding about Texans), and we didn't have to please some "foreign" group as we had with the Kenton Collection. Add to this the fact that the banks were paid off, along with a number of outside investors.

Our greatest indulgence was the "Pamper Yourself" catalogue we mailed that year, knowing it probably would not be a huge moneymaker. By now there were five buyers including myself: Margaret Anne Cullum, Jac Vroom, and Randy James had joined Allen Rushing. We decided to put out a true wish book. Everything in it would be some ultimate desire on the part of the buyers. We offered the highest-priced item Horchow has offered to date, a Coromandel screen for $60,000. It didn't sell, but it was on consignment, so we weren't out a lot of money, and I expect we established a top price we won't have to worry about for years.

Not all the "Pamper" items were near that level. Allen Rushing's ultimate desire was left over from childhood and involved all kinds of toys he hadn't been able to own as a boy. We also had Porthault sheets and pillowcases and other top-of-the-line daydreams that represent a step or two beyond "good" but aren't outrageously high-priced. We all loved the idea of the "Pamper" book. It took a lot of work, finding so much merchandise out of the usual stream of supply, so we finally broke the problem down into the five senses to establish a merchandising concept. It has remained everybody's favorite book, and through the years new buyers have begged that we do it again.

The Horchow Collection also turned to more fashions, going from 5 percent of sales in 1973 to 20 percent in 1975. One young designer who got his start with us was Andrew Downs. His first offerings were simple beach and patio robes, and they got a terrific response. An Andrew Downs gingham dress, with an elasticized top and skirt that fit any size, sold 1,500 pieces and, for a long time, was our best-selling dress ever. We were also selling Givenchy, Von Furstenberg, Clovis Ruffin, and lots of Halston.

The ownership of Horchow was now 51 percent mine, with the rest scattered among about six other persons and my children. Our five-member board included Carolyn and me; Robert Alpert of Dallas (head of Alpert Investment Corporation); my lawyer, Barney Young, also of Dallas; and my brother-in-law, Eugene Pfeifer III, of Little Rock. These people still comprise the board, and we are a congenial, close-knit group. Nobody is timid about calling my hand if there is disagreement with my decisions—it happens all the time.

I think I was lucky about my in-laws in ways completely aside from their personalities and individual worth. Carolyn's family is full of successful retail operations, and that's been helpful. Her great-grandfather Philip Pfeifer was well known in Little Rock, and on that side of her family were several Arkansas mercantile establishments: Pfeifer's, Blass, and M. M. Cohn. Her uncle Ohren Smulian operates Frougs, in Tulsa, Oklahoma, and her father and brother run the Mechanics Lumber Company in Little Rock. (Is there any wonder Carolyn went straight to work at Bloomingdale's as soon as she got out of Connecticut College in 1956?)

Early in 1975 the Horchow Collection had accumulated scores of imitators; there were half a dozen new catalogues in the mail every week. A couple of them were so obviously knockoffs of us that some of my people were getting confused. American Express brought out its first gift catalogue, and in it fifty-six items—one-third the total in the book—were the exact items we had, almost photographed the same way. It seemed very strange to me that they would pick the identical fifty-six items, and I was so incensed that I sent a letter to the president of American Express and to everybody whose name I knew that worked with their catalogue, saying that I thought they could be a little more original. Finally, after sending the letter two or three times, I got a letter back saying they were sorry I felt that way. Afterward, they never again used so many identical items.

I called everybody in for a pep rally. I went through one of the most blatantly imitative catalogues item by item and showed my workers where, and why, it wasn't really in Horchow's league.

"We don't want this kind of thing," I said, pointing to one of those cutesy bathroom items in such abominable taste, "and tell me, frankly, would any of you feel flattered if you received it as a gift? Or this . . . and this? We don't want this kind of item, which is purely for promotion and not sales, and we don't want this kind of model: him or him or her. This [pointing] isn't *ours*, or this. And people who buy this are not our customers—they are not our friends; this isn't the kind of photography we want, this isn't the grade of paper or the quality of color separation we want in our books. These people are copying us page by page, almost word by word, but let's not take it as a threat. Let's take it as flattery."

We increased apparel because our customers responded to it so wholeheartedly. A Robert Courtney dress, for instance, sold $200,000 worth in 1975. It was a dress any woman could understand, tasteful but not trendmaking. A secret, if you can call it that, of selling women's apparel by mail is to keep your selections in simple sizes: small, medium, and large, or "one size fits all." Fortunately, fashions have been somewhat on the loose, bulky side most years since we began the Collection.

We test the fit of our dresses by letting a lot of the women who work here try them on. We call it "Show & Tell," and, for every new catalogue, we have the phone operators and order takers in to try them on and see how dresses, blouses, skirts, belts, and that sort of apparel fits, so they can tell the customers if the medium, maybe, is running a bit large in this model, or that a size 12 (if it is sized) runs small. Waists and lengths are a big problem with women's wear, so we try not to offer too many things that emphasize tiny waists or long legs or short torsos. The problem is present in men's clothing, but either the clothing is standardized or men are standardized, because men's sizes mean more and are a fairly safe guide. Now and then we have trouble with a man's shirt, particularly one made in Italy or France, because it will be tight on American shoulders. The Hong Kong tailors have done a beautiful job of cutting and fitting to American sizes.

132

Apparel is chosen with the same criteria as our other merchandise. We have to think of somebody we know personally who would wear it or would like to receive it as a gift. As I said before, we'd rather have the customer feel confident in our selection than try to teach her new trends.

The return rate for ready-to-wear should be about 20 percent. That's a figure that hasn't changed much since we started. Most returns are for wrong sizes, even though the customer specified the size originally. Allen Rushing has a theory that larger-sized women in particular like to shop by mail because they can try things on at home instead of in a fitting room. We don't like returns, of course, because even when you can recycle them you've lost a lot of money in making the exchange. But the Horchow Collection has had as tolerant a returns policy as possible. And we certainly don't mind sending out another size in a $200 or $300 item.

Our computer tells us most of our customers are women, which isn't surprising, but their profile isn't at all snobbish. Many people, in and out of the industry, have taken it for granted that our customers were the people who read *Town and Country, W, Gourmet,* and *Women's Wear Daily*—the chic ladies. But a questionnaire we mailed to 100,000 persons during the fall 1978 season had some surprising answers. *Better Homes and Gardens* readers outnumbered the rest. While we have thousands of *Architectural Digest, Vogue,* and *New Yorker* subscribers among our "Horchow people," we clearly are not just an upper-class catalogue. Another thing we learned from the survey that was very interesting to us was the number of our women readers who worked. For every one hundred replies, we found fifty-three worked full time and twenty-seven part time outside their homes. That is a higher percentage of working women than we had predicted, and I think it may have crept up on us since 1974. It means the American female work force is steadily growing, but it also means you mustn't let your statistical data remain static. Especially where women are concerned.

Quite a few people who buy from the Horchow catalogues are executives with little time to spare. They make up their minds rapidly, and order with a minimum of reflection. (I suspect Horchow apparel is seen at a good many board meetings, especially on executive women.) There is quite a bit of impatience in executive types, who expect the mails to move more rapidly than is often the case. They occasionally call back within a few days of ordering, wanting to know where their order is. Executives or not, we have a word for this type inquiry: Wismo. We get a hundred or so Wismos a week, which isn't bad when you remember we process from 17,000 to 25,000 orders during that same period. Wismo means, if you haven't figured it out, "Where is my order?"

When we get a Wismo, we make a personal search for the order. We never say, "Oh, your order is on the way, it will be there soon." If we find there is a delay, even of a day or two, someone goes immediately and retrieves the Wismo and, usually within minutes, tells the customer the status of the order.

I don't mean to leave the impression that executives are the only ones who originate Wismos, and I certainly don't want to imply that all Wismos are uncalled for. Most of the time, when a customer calls about an order, the customer says, "I just wasn't sure about the mails."

I happen to have a great deal of sympathy for the postmen, having worked for the Post Office Department as a "Christmas temporary" in 1944. I started every morning around five A.M. sorting and delivering the mail. This was in the days when three and sometimes four deliveries a day were made in the holiday season. I wore out a lot of shoe leather, but I learned what kinds of mail people really wanted, and what they just accepted. The worst days were those on which the magazines came out. Many times I would have liked to throw away all the copies of *Life, Look,* and *The Saturday Evening Post.* That thought occurs to me now and then today when I wonder how my successor feels about carrying Horchow catalogues once a month. That's one reason I make sure nothing we send falls into the automatic junk-mail category. Of course, at today's rates, nothing can realistically be called junk mail. The 1978 mail-rate increase, from 7.6¢ to 8.4¢ per book, cost us an additional $300,000 in postage a year.

The typical Horchow woman is, according to our most reliable studies, well-heeled and more mature (in comparison to teen and junior shoppers), and possesses rather good taste not only in her own choices but in her choices for others. We base these conclusions, in part, on the fact that our higher priced, one-of-a-kind, and collectors items always sell out quickly and are seldom returned, either by the purchaser or a gift recipient. Another fact our questionnaire turned up was that 80 percent of our customers live in a home, as opposed to apartments or condominiums. We were somewhat surprised to learn very few own or rent second summer or winter homes. When we asked what kind of decor they had in the home, the largest number answered traditional, with eclectic second. Special decors, like Oriental, were far down the list.

Also, by 1979 our customers were located in direct proportion to the population centers; in other words, New York City, Los Angeles, and Chicago make up about the same percentage of Horchow customers as they make up the national population percentage. I believe the mail-order business (with our catalogues contributing to the shift) has gotten away from the small-town-without-a-big-store identity it had only a few years ago.

Today, convenience is the first consideration of the mail-order customer. Our Horchow woman likes to shop, but has become more and more annoyed with the major stores for their lack of good selections and the quality of attention she gets. That's what our questionnaires relate. So many salesmen act as if their job is to keep you from buying; we hear this over and over. The Horchow woman, being more mature, says she misses the attention she used to get in the better stores and doesn't get today. She is very selective, however, and would never buy her entire wardrobe from any one source. Our older customers (not in age but in number of years purchasing from us) are tremendously loyal to the Horchow catalogue. Newer customers are often fickle for a few mailings—that is, they have many places to shop before they make up their minds about the bulk of their spending. This is part of the new "catalogue generation"—and, again, something we have definitely helped to create.

People who buy from or read the catalogue regularly see themselves as a certain kind. Take twenty people who buy fairly regularly and ask them to sketch a typical Horchow customer, and they tend to draw themselves. This isn't just true of women, incidentally. Men not only see themselves as a certain kind of Horchow man, they tend to see their wives or their girlfriends as *the* Horchow woman. I know, of course, that even as you read this several of you are protesting that you don't fit the mold. But it's not the case of a mold or a lack of individuality. It's a consensus of viewpoint. Try this: Look through a catalogue and see how many of the items you would be happy to give to someone, even if you didn't particularly want or need them yourself. If you hit a high percentage of yes items, you may consider yourself "that certain Horchow kind."

There is a growing body of people who've become Horchow collectors (I can't think of a better word), who read the catalogues with an eye to the little behind-the-scenes things implied in the displays. Naturally, we love the Horchow collectors because they have become part of our "family portrait." These are the folks who write to ask if I made my appointment on April 19 ("Roger: museum board meeting 3 P.M."), or to comment that Sally, my youngest daughter, "surely is growing up"—sometimes even presuming that a dog shown in a picture is "Sister," our big black Labrador.

When we run recipes on index cards or kitchen blackboards, we always get a response from a number of readers. Once we ran a recipe which one of our artists had taken from her personal file to transcribe to an open page. In the photograph this recipe had its last line or two obscured, but we thought nothing of it. Our catalogue readers did though. We immediately got a flood of inquiries or letters chiding us for what we had done. We finally assigned one person in customer service who did nothing for several days but read the remainder of the recipe to callers.

I'm told there have been instances where customers have sent cakes or cookies baked from sample recipes in the catalogue. These never seem to make it out of the order department or the phone room, so I can't judge the results. We have become very careful about what we include in recipes or notes, but I love the idea that so many customers have this homey feeling about our operation.

In the spring of 1977, we decided to issue a new catalogue which we named Trifles, but we didn't want it to be just the Horchow catalogue under another name. We wanted to develop another taste level, but one that didn't "steal" from Horchow. The buying staff was doubtful at first. Some of us remembered the Weston Trading Co. experience. I had to do the buying for the first two Trifles books, almost on a dare. Then the other buyers relented and took over the Trifles Christmas catalogue from me. (Trifles now has its own buying staff, under director Bess Duval, and is a separate entity from the Horchow Collection.)

Allen Rushing, our former vice-president, merchandise manager, and senior buyer, found a full-page photograph in a magazine of a striking lady, shown in her finery, seated on a gold sofa with a glass of white wine in her hand, and all the buyers agreed that this had to be the Trifles wife. Randy James vowed he had, in fact, known her in Oklahoma, his home state, and Margaret Anne Cullum said our magazine lady just had to be married to a successful man named something like Michael, but called Mike. Margaret Anne says, "We decided if we could devise a Trifles family around our Trifles wife, then we could buy for that mythical family in order to distinguish the offerings from those in the Horchow catalogue."

With her glass of wine, her long legs prominently displayed, and the fresh flowers in the background, we knew the lady in the photograph had interesting taste. Her crystal didn't please everyone, neither did the pattern on her sofa—but both were obviously top of the line, or decorator's choice, for the sunroom she sat in. It was finally voted, by the buyers, that her name is G. G. (not Gigi) Westfall, and her husband is Michael Bradford Westfall, Jr. Their children are Brad III and Missy, their dog is Muffie, and their cat is Charlie. We also know her florist, her decorator, and her hairdresser. The staff is divided as to whether she lives in a San Diego suburb, Palm Beach, or Oklahoma City. In the Trifles catalogues, you may have noticed, almost everything is monogrammed GGW or MBW, and the Westfall family saga carries on. The name was researched, and there was no one of that name on our mailing list. Once the Trifles family was invented, the buyers began comparing notes on items, saying things like, "G. G. would buy that," or, "That's exactly what Mike Westfall would want for Christmas."

(I want to make clear that the woman whose picture started

it all was *not* named G. G. Westfall, and didn't live in any of the places where we think the Westfall family may live. She was merely an attractive inspiration.)

At some point, when I make a speech or am being interviewed, I will nearly always be asked some question that implies, "What's your secret?"

I have yet to find a business or a successful project of any sort which has at its heart a secret, especially a secret that will enable anyone else to copy its success. At the same time I am being asked, "What's your secret?" I also hear comments like, "Aren't you afraid you're going to tell too much?" Or, "What if your competitors find out the things you're telling?"

Well, I hereby declare, if any competitors are reading this, that these are some of my "secrets," and, if you've had to wait until now to find them out, I suspect you're not going to be a competitor much longer. On the other hand, there are enough intangibles in our operation that I have to assume there are some key things we do, and know, that no one else can do or know, regardless of what I tell.

But I will tell you how we find our merchandise, how we evaluate it, how we photograph it, and, finally, how we analyze profitability—that is, how we decide whether to repeat or drop an item and other general methods of deciding if something is making enough money or should make more.

This topic would fill a how-to book, if one is only interested in the bottom line, so I will devote a chapter to it without further ado.

XIII

My How-To Secrets

AGAIN, I WANT TO point out that following my answers will not guarantee success in the mail-order business. But I think these topics are interesting, giving readers a behind-the-scenes look at something they are familiar with from the outside.

HOW DO WE FIND OUR MERCHANDISE?

Besides our professional buyers, at least a couple of whom are always attending some trade fair or market show at any given time, we have a host of friends, relatives, and acquaintances who scout all the time. Don't underestimate them; they have been very valuable. To name a few instances: My lawyer's mother-in-law, Imogene Taylor, tipped me off about the Hoky sweeper when it was brand new to the United States. My mother-in-law, Fay Pfeifer, told me about a magic grease mop, of which we sold 20,000. Penny Rembe, of Albuquerque, New Mexico, told us about a marvelous piñon nut brittle made there, and Patricia Honea drew my attention to a superb peanut brittle made in the little town of Hamilton, Texas. My friend, Judy Cook, of Larchmont, New York, told us about a copper-and-porcelain double boiler which has turned out to be a perennial best-seller, and Bootsie Galbraith in London found a great child's safe. John Curran found a wonderful desk file which we've run for years. We listen carefully; you never know where you'll hear a great idea.

As I mentioned, my daughter Regen spotted some bandanas in twelve colors in Mexico, and they sold over five thousand dozen. Carolyn is not only a good buyer when she looks for the Collection, she uses her imagination in everyday affairs. She was irked by the ugly margarine tubs on the breakfast table, so she commissioned a plain white tub made for us in Portugal, and it, too, has been a good seller. For years Carolyn looked for some sort of portable rack that could be put up and taken down in a jiffy to use with visitors or when editing the family wardrobe. She finally uncovered one in 1978, and it was an immediate hit.

There have been many good sellers we simply have forgotten about over the years. In fact, as I am dictating this to a tape recorder, I am noticing a nice plastic birdfeeder my mother gave us some years back. It's hanging in the huge elm tree that shades my patio. We used it in the catalogue and it was a repeat seller. Maybe it should be offered again, unless there was some special reason we dropped it; maybe the manufacturer went out of business or cheap imitations took over the market. If we've simply forgotten about it (easy to do with thousands of items offered in a year's time), we may put it in the catalogue again.

Quite a few of our vendors and suppliers tell us of something unusual, often suggesting things completely out of their field, like Geoffrey Beene's suggestion of French vinegar, with which we did well, and, more recently, Mosse's Soda Bread, which he found in Ireland. And I mustn't forget my mother, who lives in Arlington, Virginia. She became associated with the national Red Cross headquarters in Washington at the beginning of World War II and for thirty-five years served in various administrative capacities in the national chapter and eastern area Red Cross until she retired in 1977. She now acts as a kind of scout for us, finding useful things she runs across in her busy life; things that our customers might like, too.

Basically, however, we find our merchandise through the talented eyes (and feet) of our buyers. We cover the major gift shows in the United States and the trade fairs of Europe, and we have commission agents in nearly every country where we buy. Horchow buyers get to the Far East each year and usually to India. They circulate around various European countries even when those countries do not have notable trade fairs. I believe we have been offered goods from just about every nation on the globe that does enough manufacturing to keep up with our demands. We have bought handmade items from the Eskimos, from Canadian Indians, from Spanish nuns (as mentioned), from isolated Mexican village craftspersons, and from Thais, Egyptians, and Tibetans ... and we were among the early buyers from the United States to visit the People's Republic of China when that trade door reopened.

As I write this, the most interesting items we are offered in China are antique pieces: old silver, porcelain, and jade. Chinese basketry is still wonderful, though now commonplace. Chinese merchants, or heads of government bureaus that handle merchandise, are quick to catch sales trends. They raised their prices quickly after the first wave of American buyers found their goods were bargains. But because there is (at this time) so little individual responsibility, things like guarantees, packing, and breakage are mostly just a matter of hope. You don't have much recourse. I am hoping this situation will get better as the United States and China enter into closer trade and diplomatic ties.

On the other hand, trying to do business with Russia, on the product level, is often an even more exasperating experience. While the Chinese are not producing much new, they can at least fill orders when you sign a contract for something at a Canton or a Peking exhibit. But when Allen spotted some exquisite lacquer boxes and nested dolls at the Russian booth at the Frankfurt Trade Fair in West Germany one year, he tried to buy enough to feature them in our catalogue. "I'm sorry," the Russian exhibitor told him, "our production is entirely sold out . . . in fact, we have been sold out for over a month."

"Why are you showing them at the fair?" Allen wanted to know—especially since the Frankfurt Fair was in its very first day.

"Oh, they just told me to come and bring some things, and these are very pretty," the Russian said. (We later got some nested dolls—but only when the Russians were ready, not when we tried to order them first.)

We also are shown a tremendous amount of merchandise from manufacturers who come to us with new ideas—fortunately, we have achieved a reputation so that we get first-look at a great many things. We also go through a couple of dozen foreign magazines looking for items that might be adapted to the U.S. market, or new things we can get more quickly by ordering direct rather than by waiting for the usual trade channels. It doesn't really matter much whether we can read the language of the magazines; if something can sell itself strictly by picture, so much the better.

We also make adaptations of old items, we commission new designs and patterns, and we update certain items that sold well in the past. As it is almost impossible to protect a design, once it's in the market, we are constantly redesigning our own best-sellers when others have done knockoffs—the trade term for copying some successful piece of goods.

One of the best-selling items in the 1975 Christmas catalogue came to me from my youngest daughter, Sally. Her favorite Christmas present the year before had been a small mechanical savings bank. Watching her play with it, I thought to myself, "If little Sally likes that so much at age four, why wouldn't a whole lot more children and adults want the same thing?" We searched around until we found the manufacturer, chose a new color scheme (a zippy red, white, and blue motif in anticipation of the U.S. Bicentennial), and wound up selling 22,000 of them at $7.50.

HOW DO WE EVALUATE THE MERCHANDISE ONCE WE HAVE A SAMPLE?

We have a list of requirements which I believe are of interest to anyone who buys from a catalogue. Most are self-explanatory:

- Is it a good value?
- Will it give us enough profit?
- Is it a straightforward, honest item?
- Is it of good quality? (We want to protect the customer, first of all, but, also, we don't want to have to take a lot of merchandise back because it is poorly made or of inferior material.)
- Is it easy to pack and ship? (I should say, can it be made to fit; we have to pack and ship lots of things that aren't *easy*.)
- Is there a lot of competition on the item? (We don't like to copy others.)
- Will it be understood from a photograph? (Stationery, for example, does not sell well from photographs.)
- Is it a sensible item or would it be used just to create a sensational image? (We don't do any "His and Hers" type offerings for glamor only; we leave that to others.)
- Have we had anything like it before to which we may compare sales potential?

- If not, is it worth trying?
- Will it be exclusive to the Horchow Collection?
- Is it important to us that it be exclusive?
- If it is not exclusive, where else will it be sold?
- How long will we be allowed to have the item before it is sold to the general market?
- If it is clothing, will there be a size problem, or will one size fit all?
- Can we explain how it fits, or works, in our copy or over the telephone? (We simply can't say, "Oh, you'll just have to try it and see.")

WHAT ABOUT OUR SUPPLIERS?

Knowing the supplier is tremendously important, and, after our customer list, I might rate our supplier list next in value. Our list of requirements here is also rather full:

- Is the supplier reliable?
- Will we be able to get reorders?
- Have we had previous experience with the supplier?
- Will the item being offered sell a minimum of $7,000 or more at retail? (This figure, as explained, moves up with inflation.)
- If we don't sell all we buy, would the supplier allow us to return unsold goods?

Sometimes, of course, we will take something that doesn't pass all the above requirements but looks like a reasonably good gamble. (Supplier reorder capability and that minimum-sales figure are probably the most hard-and-fast requirements.) Jac Vroom once recommended we sell a calculator/clock radio/alarm combination at $100, and I told him, "You're crazy. That price is double what the rest of the market gets." Jac defended his choice by pointing out that the qualities this appliance offered, the lower end couldn't touch. I reluctantly accepted his pitch. He persuaded the Art Department to devote a full page to the calculator/clock radio/alarm item and he went to the copywriter to explain all its functions. It turned out to be a wonderful best-seller.

Another amusing example of my misgivings concerns a feather duster. When a feather duster was presented for a special household book we did a few years back, I laughed wickedly and said no one had used a feather duster since 1898, not even my grandmother in Zanesville. But, trying to be as open-minded as possible, I allowed it to run. It turned out to be an all-time favorite. It's still running. Carolyn explained to me that there are hundreds of things you can't reach with a vacuum cleaner attachment, or things you mustn't trust to a heavy brush in the human hand. Museums use feather dusters all the time. We have now sold at least 12,000 of this handy but old-fashioned device, because it still works better than any substitute.

HOW DO WE CHOOSE ONE ITEM OVER ANOTHER?

Sometimes we carry samples right down to the wire, hoping to find a reasonable economic excuse to include them in a catalogue, and we'll earmark one for some special book in the future if that's possible. We start with the time of year or the season, then ask questions like these:

- Does the item fit a certain catalogue theme?
- Is there too much duplication of this type merchandise in one catalogue? Too many earrings ... salad bowls ... robes ... mugs?
- Is this item costlier to pack than another we are looking at?
- Will freight and mailing expense to the customer be too great compared to the cost of the merchandise?
- Does the item still look as good as it did when we first saw it? (Disillusionment can come easily, especially when you take into consideration that the catalogue for which the item is being considered may not be scheduled for six or eight months.)

- Have we seen similar new items in other mail-order catalogues we had not known about before? (In other words, are we the last to know?)
- Has something in our thinking changed between the time we first saw the merchandise and the time we have finished selecting for the book? (This could be anything from a sudden swerve in fashion to an unpleasant episode with a designer or manufacturer, or a lawsuit or threat of a lawsuit.)
- Is this really the best moment to run this particular item? (Some news event may have made it inappropriate—we have to be careful about such things as certain leathers, ivory, or feathers—or the cost may skyrocket; late in 1979, in one day the cost, to us, of gold jumped 40 percent, which meant our prices had to move up even more to cover that added cost.)
- Was the sample on time and was it the right size and color? (We always say that if the supplier cannot get the sample to us as promised, then it's likely he will also fail later on the order.)
- Have we picked too many items for this particular catalogue?

We have been complimented consistently on our artwork and presentation of items. In fact, if there is an area where our competitors have failed most noticeably, I think it is here—in the look and image—the ambience—of our catalogue. As one old merchandising expert said when our first Trifles catalogue was distributed, "I read the first page and knew, without looking further, it was 'Horchow.'"

We have an in-house art staff and our photographers are based in Dallas. After we select the items for the catalogue, we give our art staff our ideas, tell them why we chose the item, and ask them to prepare a preliminary page breakdown. Together, we may select certain themes—such as the seasons, travel, art, Christmas tree decorations, cooking equipment—or sometimes a subtle theme that's whimsical, like a motif featuring frogs or some other animal.

We frequently select items to be given great prominence based on large purchase and good profitability, or an unusual kind of purchase. One-of-a-kind, high-priced items are usually given this same treatment. We also let Vona McDonald and Larry Jennings, our Art Directors, select items which might have special appeal, basing the choice on the general look of the specific book, or simply going on some creative idea of the art staff. In this respect, the art staff has a wide latitude.

When we photograph items in a studio or a home, we do not use famous backgrounds, neither do we take our models and cameras halfway around the globe just to shoot in an exotic setting. We're not trying to sell visits to Venice or trips to Tripoli.

Models are very important, and we try to match the item with the model, especially if it is an expression of personality, like children playing with toys. We have special models for hands, feet, necks, even ears. Most of our models are professionals from Dallas. Dallas has become such an important international fashion center that getting the best models and photographers there is no problem. All three of my daughters and Carolyn have been used as models in our catalogue from time to time because they filled a certain need and were available. I have also used friends' children both as a gesture of friendship and because the children looked good in pictures. No matter whom we finally choose as the model, we ask in advance what the model should look like and what kind of person would be wearing the clothes that we are showing.

We pay careful attention in the layouts not only to the offering but to all the other items and props shown with it. When dishes are offered, we try to have placemats and napkins that are available from us, or of our level of quality and taste. Our readers scrutinize each picture, some using magnifying glasses to "read" stitches or fine handwriting on notes.

Because we have been copied by many other U.S. catalogues, we have changed our format from time to time, although very slightly in most cases. One year I decided to switch from all photographs to some sketches. In a summertime specialty catalogue for cooks, the sketched items sold very well, so I told the Art Department to use more sketches in our Christmas books. I should have tested further; the sketched items did not generally sell well at Christmas because I chose the wrong items for sketching.

Beginning in 1979, we made some radical changes in our format and artwork because I felt that all the mail-order catalogues were becoming alike. While ours had its own aura, that aura had been copied to the point it was no longer ours. Rip the cover off most catalogues and they swam together in your mind. As a customer, I had reached the point where, curious as I am, I found it difficult to go through every catalogue. My first reaction was (and remains so most of the time), "Ugh . . . another copy of our book." I found myself thinking, "This turns me against my own catalogue."

HOW ABOUT PROFITABILITY?

Since each customer averages two items per order, we have to take the overall sales and the overall costs to get an average profit picture per order. When we finish selling it, we analyze each item as follows:

- What was the size of our order?
- What was the gross profit in dollars from the original sale?
- What was the cost of handling that specific item?
- What was the allocation of overhead to that item?
- How much leftover merchandise remains, if any, because of incorrect buying?
- How much price reduction, overall, did it take to sell the remaining merchandise?

Sometimes we are willing to pay for the lesson by wasting space in a catalogue to see if a specific type item will sell by mail—we did this on lithographs (original), tennis racquets, and expensive jigsaw puzzles. We also test to find out if some item might sell just as well in black-and-white as in color, or in a sketch rather than a photograph. Certain items "carry" as well in monochrome as color, for example, our famous ice cream scoop, my beloved glass dessert sets, dominoes—even the feather duster I initially feared.

Part of the profitability of any item relates to the amount sent back by our customers. We have a very liberal returns policy: If you are not completely satisfied, we will accept the prompt return of any item except personalized items and sale items. I'm sure a great many readers wonder how badly this policy gets abused. There have been a few persons who sent back merchandise they had almost worn out (we've had to literally burn a few of the items of clothing) or have deliberately ordered things they had no intention of keeping. A woman from Michigan constantly ordered dresses, returning them a month later, complaining they weren't as pictured in the catalogue, or that she disliked the material—any excuse except wrong size, or something else we might be able to take care of. It didn't take long to realize the woman was using a revolving wardrobe free of charge from Horchow. Eventually we told her, gently, that we thought it best she not try to buy Horchow items since they never pleased her. We refused to ship further orders to her, and was she furious!

SHOULD WE REPEAT OR DROP AN ITEM?

We keep lists of the twenty-five best-sellers by dollar sales and the twenty-five best-sellers by units sold. We try to analyze why the item was a good seller—was it the season, the price, the layout and picture, a suggested use, or its newness? Should we repeat it?

We repeat ten to fifteen of the items that appear on the

best-seller list if such items are still available and are still timely. Obviously, we can't repeat a best-selling Christmas ornament in February or a summer robe in January. Sometimes a very big seller has a limited life, particularly in fashion. The biggest dollar volume we have had on a single item, to date, was a Molly Parnis Ultrasuede shirtdress for $260 featured in our Christmas 1977 catalogue. We sold over 1,300 dresses for a retail sale of $350,000. But we couldn't repeat it.

In some cases a price increase will stop us from repeating a good seller. A certain pair of Cartier gold ball cufflinks was a sensational seller at $60 a pair, then did rather well when the rising cost of gold forced the price to $100. But $300 per pair finally stopped the sale. Gold has kept on rising.

If we repeat an item more than once we consider it to be a "Collection Classic." We never drop an item as long as it is a winner and available. We keep our repeat merchandise together, in most catalogues, marking the section "Collection Classics." Examples are our ice cream scoop with built-in antifreeze to make it usable on hard ice cream, my glass dessert set, a toy helicopter, the "Carolyn" notepad and holder, a child's "hero helmet," a silver dripless wine spout, simple magnifying reading glasses, a stapleless stapler, our signature shoe protectors, and Carolyn's porcelain margarine dish. Not all of these are repeated in the same book, but you will find them offered from one book to the next. The ice cream scoop and the dessert set are in almost every catalogue except the specialty books.

An item is removed from "Collection Classics" when sales finally slow down to the point where it no longer meets the minimum sale requirement. (Some of the items I listed above may have been removed by now.) Sometimes the buyers get tired of an item (they want to have fresh ideas), but, from a practical standpoint, one must never forget the basic items which the customers identify as their favorites. When it becomes impossible to repeat them, one must keep an eye open for new adaptations or improved models—as in the case of the Cuisinart food processor. Certain items break, or wear out, yet the desire for them is still strong and new customers and new generations of buyers come along. For instance, many customers have ordered as many as ten separate sets of the dessert dishes.

XIV

Hummers and Bummers

I KNOW THAT SOME OF you are saying to yourself, "He doesn't always win," and you are right. Despite our best judgment and despite a continuing amount of experience, we hit a loser now and then—more *then* than *now*, I'm relieved to state. The order department has a set of terms for success and failure among our merchandise. Something that takes off immediately and sells above expectations or predictions is a *hummer*. An item that does the opposite, or has lots of headaches attached to the handling of it, is a *bummer*. Most of our real bummers have happened when we did something against our better judgment.

I guess my most famous bummer was a leather ice bucket shaped like a pumpkin "which never did turn into a coach," as a Washington *Post* feature writer remarked. One of my (admitted) weaknesses is taking the word of friends when they are enthusiastic on the spur of the moment. I was introduced to a Bavarian prince at a small party at the home of a famous Dallas decorator. The prince was reputed to be the most creative man in the Western Hemisphere, with a factory down in

Mexico where he turned out beautiful objects. I must have been swept away by the glamor of the evening (I really don't imbibe very much) because I was talked into buying one hundred of his pumpkin-shaped and pumpkin-colored ice buckets to retail at $150.

I told glowing tales to the staff about what a marvelous ultimate luxury gift the bucket would make, and how it would be a Horchow exclusive. Everyone was keyed up, waiting to see the dazzling creature. Well, when the sample finally arrived, we discovered the bucket held only about twelve ice cubes. Then, a parade of small, but significant, misadventures set in (the late arrival of the sample should have alerted me), we had a hard time with delivery, and the quality differed throughout the run.

But, more important, nobody wanted to buy the foolish buckets, and I was committed to one hundred of them. We sold about six through the catalogue initially, although most of these came back with letters that, quite often, gave far too explicit instructions about disposing of them. We then offered the buckets in a sale catalogue and got about forty takers. Somebody on the staff proposed taking a knife to the remainder and offering them as the most expensive jack-o'-lanterns in America, but I said no—it was too long to wait until Halloween. Some of the pumpkin ice buckets even survived our gigantic Garage Sale, and I urged everyone to use them around the office for any purpose for which they could be accommodated (they were too small for a trash basket and too large for an ashtray.) I still keep one in my sample closet as a reminder of my good judgment.

Our all-time loser in dollars was a black velvet party dress for girls, which we had especially made for us in England by a French dressmaker to whom Fleur Cowles introduced me. When I talked to this dressmaker, it was agreed the dress would be ready for the Christmas season, and, in order to be sure subsequent orders would be filled quickly, I also agreed to purchase quite a bit of additional velvet cloth. Our initial order was for five hundred dresses, to sell for $35 each.

To make a sad story short, the velvet party dresses didn't get shipped in time for the Christmas catalogue, and we offered them in the January book. We sold seventy-five, and I went into a frenzy. This dress had *everything* going for it, I thought: handmade in London by a French dressmaker, a lovely little-girl design in luscious velvet, and at an unusually reasonable price.

Carolyn, who hadn't been in on the transaction, analyzed the problem in a few sentences. "Roger," she said, when I told her the dress was a disaster, "for the father of three daughters, you have a lot to learn. The only time anyone buys velvet party dresses for girls is *before* Christmas. It won't do any good to put them on sale. The calendar's against you."

She was right. We offered the dress in a sale book but only sold a few more. I finally donated the remainder to a children's home. The last I saw of this bummer was a notation from the bookkeeper that we had "500 pounds of velvet." I didn't ask if it was avoirdupois or pounds sterling.

On the other hand, we have learned a few things about backing up our orders. Not long ago I dispatched two buyers to fly to Hong Kong (at a cost of $5,000) to persuade a manufacturer to make more and more of a $46 oatmeal-colored sweater after we had gotten 4,500 orders for it from a holiday preview book. The buyers thought I was crazy when I placed the original order for $25,000 worth of the sweaters—but they were out cheering when the new shipment arrived at the freight dock in time to fill that avalanche of orders.

The lesson one should learn about celebrity-promoted products is that the product must be looked at in relation to the price of similar products, no matter how famous the person may be who makes it. I had just the opposite experience to my adventure with the Bavarian prince when I met Diane von Furstenberg. Although she was Princess von Furstenberg, she knew the realities of the business world. She offered us a specific type of dress at a very reasonable price, and after meeting her and discussing the sale of her dresses through our mail-order catalogue, we hit upon a style and color we both thought would be appropriate—and we sold 1,200 of them at $68 per dress.

In the early days of business I was more receptive to (and impressed by) celebrities, believing that even if I only broke even in profit-and-loss on their products I would be ahead because of the prestige of their names. I confess, too, that royalty has a certain charm which comes, I suppose, from so many of them having to hustle their way through life during the past two hundred years that they have been out of office. At any rate, after our very satisfactory experience with Diane von Furstenberg, we were a little more receptive to nobility, and in this case the Princess led us to the Baron ... no, let me restate that: the Bar-ON. Princess Diane told me that her dear friend, the Baron A. de R. from Paris was making fantastic backgammon sets and since backgammon was *the* rage (at that time) and was the game of kings, we certainly ought to have the sets—and if we were going to have them they ought to come from the Bar-ON.

Well, the Bar-ON appeared in our lives, and, with his great enthusiasm and charm, convinced me and partially convinced some of our buyers that we should run a special mailing of his sets around Christmas time. He gave us name after name of every celebrity we'd ever heard of, from his *dear* friend Liza Minelli, to his *old pal* Jack Haley, to Count this and Contessa that, plus a hundred or so other movie and television stars. . . . "It will be simply a matter of you finding the addresses," he assured us.

We worked to get the brochure produced in the kind of exquisite taste he required, and (orchestrating the whole thing) he insisted we also show his $20,000 backgammon table of which he was certain we would sell many. After I began writing down the numbers, the investment came to several hundred thousand dollars on my part, and I finally put my foot down and bought many fewer than he suggested.

But more than I should have, it turned out. It had been a real struggle to keep from buying that $20,000 table, I will admit, because I was convinced the Bar-ON knew what he was talking about and it would be sold, possibly in quantity, to some of those famous friends. Reality hit swiftly and hit hard. We found we were selling almost the same backgammon sets as others and were paying almost twice as much just to have the Bar-ON's seal on them. As for that expensive backgammon table, the only friend who wanted it was a celebrity whose name shall be unmentioned, who wanted it for half price, since he knew the Bar-ON . . . and, even then, I'm not sure he was serious.

After the backgammon experience, the Horchow organization retreated to its crass commercial world and we redevoted our attention and time to quality of product and not quality of bloodlines of the designer.

I have an adage which is, unfortunately, too long to put on a doormat, a cocktail glass, or even a wall plaque. But it should be memorized by all retail business persons: If you have trouble getting the sample, you will have trouble getting the merchandise, or, put another way, if something begins with trouble, it will never straighten out.

The more innocent the problem may seem, the more intricate the tangle will become. A perfect example of this was my commercial dealings with designer Piero Fornasetti of Milan. Many years ago at Neiman–Marcus we carried a lot of the works of Signor Fornasetti during an Italian Fortnight. At the time, I was the new gift buyer and one of the things I had not learned was when you could talk back to the boss. So, as the Fornasetti merchandise poured in, I simply gritted my teeth, feeling it would not sell but assuming the boss wouldn't want to hear my doubts.

As the years went on, I started asserting myself, and, when Fornasetti sent samples which I had not really requested, I prepared a memo in the back of my mind to be careful when dealing with him. Once he sent a $2,500 faux-malachite-covered desk and said that Stanley Marcus had admired it and wanted it in the Gift Department. If it had come when I was first on the job, I probably would have accepted it without question, but by then I was asking questions. It turned out Mr. Marcus had admired it but hadn't placed an order, and he was as upset as I was to see it arrive for stock.

Years passed, lives changed, and twelve years later I revisited Signor Fornasetti, thinking it might be a good time to revive some of his beautiful merchandise. I saw some faux-malachite plates at his Milan outlet and ordered them for our 1974 Christmas catalogue. They arrived in the United States and were immediately confiscated by the Food and Drug Administration which insisted the plates contained too much lead and could never be sold in the United States for food service. This was not quite as quick in happening as I have told it, and we had to refund all our customers' money, after having had long correspondence while we were waiting for the FDA decision.

We then petitioned the FDA to allow us to sell the malachite plates as ashtrays. We were given permission to do so, *providing* we showed them in our catalogue with a cigarette in them, and had a sticker printed to paste on the bottom of the plate stating they should never be used for food because they were poisonous and could be injurious to one's health. We had the stickers printed (worded as required), and we photographed the former plates as ashtrays, and came out owning twelve times more ashtrays than I would have liked: We had to divide each dozen malachite plates into units of one ashtray.

The next thing we knew, the government told us we had called the plate-ashtrays hand-painted, and they were not. We replied that Fornasetti said they were. The government said they weren't, whether Fornasetti said they were or not didn't matter. So, again, we removed them from sale and, again, started corresponding with our new set of customers who had bought them as ashtrays, telling them the shipment would be held up some more.

After new stickers were placed on the plate-ashtrays stating they were injurious to health, poisonous, only to be used as ashtrays, and were not hand-painted but, rather, the pattern was a decal (applied by hand) . . . we were allowed to sell them. I'm sure I don't have to tell you that most of them were returned by customers who, having read all the warnings, decided they didn't like them after all. If only we had allowed the FDA to confiscate them and destroy them in the first place, we would have been ahead of the game.

XV

Lists of Secrets
and Vice Versa!

I'M SURE THAT TALK
about "bummers" and awkward moments of ordering and not
selling has caused you to wonder what we do about losers and
leftover inventory. One of the benefits of mail-order business is
that you have a good order flow and don't have to keep too
high an inventory to back up sales. But that doesn't mean you
can hold several hundred thousands, or several millions, of
dollars worth of goods in the warehouse from one year to the
next. Inventory control is one of the major keys to success and
survival. As I have said, the best inventory control is how you
buy, but timidity in ordering can cost you as much as having
an inventory carry-over if you lose too great a proportion of
sales because you didn't buy aggressively enough.

Sometimes, though, we have a lot of merchandise left over
which includes some very successful items we won't offer
again. We've made money from selling the items because we

had sufficient stock to cover even the unexpected orders, but we have too many pieces left on hand or too many dollars invested. In such cases we put the merchandise in a sale book, which we issue about once every eighteen months. We price our sale goods at approximately half the original catalogue price (sometimes even lower) and give our regular customers a chance at them.

In 1976 we opened an outlet store in Dallas called "Horchow Collection Finale" where we offered leftover catalogue goods at half-price or so, along with a small amount of damaged goods which we found impossible to put back in tip-top shape. This outlet was an instant success. After the first year of operation, we could see this Finale store was a simple and profitable way to relieve inventory excess, and the shoppers, many of whom had never bought from the catalogue, loved it. By the end of 1978, we had opened a store in nearby Fort Worth and a second Finale store in Dallas.

My buying staff usually votes, after the sales of each catalogue are recorded, an item that was the worst bummer of the book. It's called the "Fruitcake Award," and no one is immune. We all like to think that anything we choose for the catalogue will be a decent seller, and competition for "Collection Classics" is fraught with pride, but there are some reverse classics no one likes to remember. One item no one will admit to buying is an Italian-designed table lamp which we offered at $360 a few years back. Thank heavens we ordered in moderation, because we sold one-fifth our projection. As you can see, the "Fruitcake Award" is made for the worst sellers, not just for questionable picks. (Who *did* buy that lamp . . . could it have been . . . *I?*)

Usually, when being interviewed by some publication, I am asked if I am a mail-order customer myself. I certainly am, even with a warehouse full of goods at my disposal. I became a mail-order customer long before I owned my own mail-order business. I do some mail-order shopping to keep up with other catalogues and their services, but I also do it because it's convenient and satisfactory—and it still gives me a thrill to get packages. At this moment, for instance, I am wearing khaki pants, a sweater, a shirt, socks, and underwear, all of which came by way of mail order. And these loafers I have on aren't Gucci's. They're the classic penny loafers by Bass Weejuns which are offered in our catalogue. But I'll admit, I didn't order them by mail. I got them out of stock.

I don't mind admitting we have bummers and have made mistakes that cause wise merchandisers to shake their heads in astonishment. I don't mind having an unhappy customer tell me some beautiful item is ugly or that an exquisite piece is of inferior taste. That's a personal choice. What I do deplore, however, is the person who lumps all catalogue mailings into the "junk mail" category. To me, junk mail is something that comes uninvited and unwanted, offering something or some service either useless or annoying to the sensibilities of the receiver. At today's postal rates, it is hard to imagine anyone sending true junk mail by means of random lists. A mail-order firm would have to be out of its mind to spend the enormous amount of postage and list-rental expenses on a blanket mailing that might include any significant number of people who would object to the offering.

In the beginning we used charge account names from Cartier, Jensen, Mark Cross, and other Kenton Corporation companies for our base mailing, but we rented millions of names from other mail-order companies. These are arranged for through list brokers. They are an entire industry, separate from, yet related to, mail order. When we need to rent names, we call the list broker to place the order for names to rent or exchange. These names can only be used once, and each list owner plants fake names in his list before it is rented to assure its being used only once. If a renter ever violates this trust, he can be boycotted by all mailers and never allowed to rent names again.

By now the Horchow mailing list is virtually 100 percent by request. We spent thousands of dollars building up a mailing list, but within a few years we had narrowed it down to names of people who actually bought from us or who had asked that they be added to our catalogue mailings. Our mailing list is the most precious asset of the Horchow organization, even though we have warehouses full of valuable goods. The list is computerized and we have access, in seconds, to how many customers live in specific cities or zip codes, when an individual ordered and how much was spent for the order, and, in some cases, if the customer might have special charge or shipping instructions. We also have a kind of self-cleaning system which removes names that have not responded in a certain number of catalogue mailings, and, when applicable, removes names which have been duplicated. Our list was developed with the costly blood of experience, and, in case of a disaster, I would try to grab my list before anything else in the building.

We have in the past made our customer list available to carefully screened companies and organizations whose products and activities might be of interest to our customers. The selection of companies to whom we rent our lists must always be approved by me. Our rental list charges are much more expensive than other catalogues, so cheaper catalogue mailers seldom tried to rent ours; we have also turned down many requests to rent our lists because I felt the firm or products were not acceptable.

I want to go into this business of renting names as thoroughly as possible because it is one question about the mail-order business that is on a lot of people's minds. Why do we do it? First, it is profitable to rent lists to others as it helps keep our costs as low as possible. If we exchange names with other mail-order catalogues, it helps us add new names to our mailing lists which helps offset the names we lose each year for one reason or another.

We decided in 1979 to stop renting our list of names to competitors because we feel the marketplace is overflowing with catalogues and we no longer wish to further that saturation. Prior to the January 1979 catalogue, our books carried the note that if you didn't want your name rented, all you had to do was notify our "mail preference service" and your name would not be rented or exchanged with others. We mail approximately one million copies of each catalogue, and most years that will run close to twenty-five million documents. Out of all those mailings, we had fewer than 550 requests to keep a name from being rented or exchanged.

Today, with so many of us subscribing to magazines and getting merchandise by mail, it is often hard to figure out how your name got on some list. An easy way to tell where your name came from is if there is a misspelling of it or a mistake in the address. For example, my name (from one list) has the street name rolled together like this: Goldhill. On another list there's this misspelling: Hirchow. When I see these mistakes on a new mailing, I immediately know where that list originated. Frequently, when I buy something, I'll order as "Roger L. Horchow" or "Samuel R. Horchow"; then I always know where the list started and how often others use my name.

I have a flexible policy about requests for charities. I give everyone a hearing and the only times I say no is when the charity can only help a very few persons—or I have reason to think it may be fraudulent. (I am not writing this to make Roger Horchow sound like a philanthropist, but I hope others may see how a corporation can function in what I feel is a responsible way toward its public obligations. I think each of us—but especially those of us in business—has an obligation to the community, to the nation, and to humanity.)

Often we make special efforts on behalf of some worthwhile undertaking. In 1976 we commissioned (and Susan Benjamin of Halcyon Days in London designed) five Bilston and Battersea enamel boxes to mark the U.S. Bicentennial. We then donated $20,000 from the sale to the American Institute for Public Service. (I am a board member of this organization, founded to create a Nobel-type prize for public service in the United States.) Before that, we had taken two Sesame Street puzzles and packaged them together, selling them with a note which told customers that a portion of the proceeds was going to be donated to the Children's Television Workshop.

Over the years we have been able to contribute several thousand dollars to the World Wildlife Fund–U.S., either from commissioning appropriate works or by donating a portion of proceeds from the sale of certain wildlife-related items.

Not all our benevolent works turn out well. Any company that attempts to be responsible to the public at large finds itself in the position of being taken from time to time. However, it has happened to us surprisingly few times. Once we got taken right at our back door, literally. There is an annual charity auction in Dallas which uses goods and services donated by all sorts of manufacturers, merchandisers, and individuals. One year I was called by a woman whom I knew and asked to contribute merchandise for the auction. I asked my secretary to put together $2,000 worth or so of goods and told her whom to contact.

Using the phone number supplied her, my secretary told the person on the other end of the line that our contribution could be picked up at any time but that it was rather sizable. Two weeks went by and my secretary (a very efficient person who loathes inefficiency) was concerned that no one had come to gather the goods. She called the number again and a woman who answered said she would be right out. That afternoon my secretary noticed the packages had been removed.

In about a week I got a call from the first woman, my friend, diplomatically inquiring if Horchow were going to honor its commitment. I said the goods had been picked up, and gave her the name of the woman who had said she was in charge of accumulating things for the auction. A short while later, my friend called back and said the woman in question had not gotten the merchandise. No one ever found who picked up over $2,000 worth of auction gifts. It was a very cool, but brazen, theft.

Some readers, I am sure, wonder if this charity I've described "begins at home." I think it does. The Horchow organization not only pays better-than-average wages, but, for permanent employees, has a generous profit-sharing plan. An added benefit in working for Horchow is that our hours are staggered in so many directions that even a part-time worker can virtually pick the hours to work. Our telephone-order room operates twenty-four hours a day, seven days a week, and our mail-order department starts work at 6 A.M. These hours mean a lot to people who live in the country and get up early or who have to get up with a spouse who has an early job in downtown Dallas. They come in early and work for us and are through in plenty of time to be home when the kids get back from school, do the chores, or have supper fixed for the family.

I might point out an amusing sidelight of the Horchow location. Although our mailing address is Dallas, this luxury item, high-fashion organization is actually in Farmers Branch, a suburban town on the northwestern edge of Dallas—so we live in the country, too.

I suppose it's not necessary to say that our company has no racial or age restrictions. In fact, we're famous for hiring people in their seventies or even eighties. Age eighty-three is our record, I believe. Our order processing department is very popular with the elderly, the displaced homemakers, and women (mainly) who have reared a family and want to do something profitable with their newly discovered time. The work is not strenuous or high-pressure, and it is conducted under pleasant conditions. In fact, you find a high level of retired professionals and others with different work experience now working for us. We have few restrictions and we let the employees do the work the way they want to; consequently, we get a happy, loyal group throughout the organization. At this time we have about 250 persons on the permanent staff; this figure increases to as many as six hundred workers during the Christmas ordering season.

We try to consider the individual in our dealings. A buyer or I will read every letter that comes in suggesting lines or offering products, and the small entrepreneur gets the same consideration as a large manufacturer who wants a spot in our catalogue. This means we do not accept subsidies or cooperative advertising in our catalogues—which is a way a manufacturer or supplier can pay to get his goods displayed as he chooses in many other catalogues. We don't want to give up control of our book. We only negotiate for quantity discounts or advertising allowances with no strings attached, and only *after* we have made up our minds what will be carried. With subsidies and cooperative ads, catalogues can actually make money in themselves for the company that issues them, by featuring products by brand names. Have you ever wondered why a simple description of a dress or robe must sound so complicated? Each of the trade names—fabric, thread, knitting process—is paying something for the privilege of being mentioned and adds, I think, little to help a customer decide to buy.

Whatever is included in a Horchow catalogue, we are responsible for, and we make all the decisions involving how much space to devote to it and where it is to be displayed. Some catalogues, especially store catalogues, don't do this.

However, I don't want to give the impression that subsidies and co-op ads are unethical. They are a common, accepted practice in retailing and are a big source of income to some retailers.

It is often simpler to deal with an established manufacturer or a big importer, but I learned early that the minute you get too rigid, so that you can't adjust to the first-time or the untrained vendors, you are in trouble. That's why there are always more people, including artists and craftspersons, trying to see me on my New York trips (every two months, at least) than I can possibly see. But I try never to leave anyone dangling; if I can't see them, I am willing to set up a meeting for next trip, and the buyers, or our merchandising manager, will talk to everyone, literally, who wants to come to our Dallas headquarters and make an appointment with someone who is free.

Don't think we never get tough with suppliers, or that we won't push for a bargain or a discount with the trade. We have started several craft and design careers, but we have done it because we felt we were doing a service for our customers and could make a profit as well. When I tell about learning lessons, I hope my readers can read between the lines and know that I try not to have to learn them over and over. In other words, we are flexible, but we aren't fragile.

I like the idea that some effort on my part, whether a personal decision or a corporate project, can be productive and profitable—and at the same time help improve the image of public service and responsibility. At the present time I think this is best maintained in my role as a responsive businessman and private citizen, but I have always been interested in the mechanics of politics. I guess it began when I lived in Washington, D.C. You can't live in Washington without recognizing the tremendous power politics has to change lives. In some areas, politics is the *only* thing that can make these changes.

When I first met Jimmy Carter, he impressed me very favorably. Our January 1977 catalogue featured peanut-motif items and some friends asked me if I hadn't taken a big gamble, knowing I had to order the peanut items as far back as April of the year before, several months before Jimmy Carter even got the nomination. Actually, in my enthusiasm I had thought of putting a peanut on the catalogue cover, but then I reconsidered. At least half our customers are Republican and no matter how enthusiastic I might be, there was no sense offending them. The Horchow Company, after all, was not supporting Carter; Roger Horchow was. I pointed out to critics that the catalogue copy for a peanut-print scarf talks about it having "an elephant gray" border, so it was actually a bipartisan item.

For a while I made no secret of my wish to become Undersecretary of Commerce under President Carter. In fact, I had wanted to be in Commerce well before I knew Carter's name. My friend Larry McQuade's time as an Assistant Secretary of Commerce was the inspiration for that desire. However, I took a hard look at my life and the lives of my family, and decided that, whatever my ambitions might be, I couldn't take the time, for now anyway, so I didn't pursue that goal.

But, I will admit, I would like to be Secretary of Commerce someday, just because I think the post would benefit from someone who has been in commerce. I am not criticizing anyone who holds an office in the Department of Commerce, but I think a lot of good could come from having a person in that sensitive position who has done business with Japan while the dollar was falling, or who has suffered because of badly thought out import quotas and restrictions. I know from experience that American competition is global, and, when we try to give any special industry a protective wall, we can easily damage more American commerce than that we are trying to protect. And, on the other hand, when an American opportunity does arise, someone should be on the scene who can quickly recognize it and do something with it.

Early in 1979, I decided to do something. The U.S. dollar had weakened all over the world in the face of certain currencies. I decided this would be a good time to really study the international market and see if U.S.-made goods hadn't gotten into an excellent competitive position; where once it was cheaper to buy foreign-made items because of the strength of the dollar, maybe it was as cheap, or cheaper, now to "buy American."

We assembled our "Buy American" catalogue and issued it July 4, 1979, with a tasteful "All American" cover. Everything in the book was U.S.-made. The prices were competitive with foreign costs and the quality was competitive or superior. I think our gesture was a great success. It pointed out the new possibilities of U.S. manufacturing arts and it led to more retail concentration on our nation's products. Not that I would start a boycott on foreign goods—we're still globe-trotting buyers—but perhaps a realistic movement to purchase at home can make U.S. products more visible.

Our Commerce Department could then use this very understandable and visual presentation of the best consumer goods made in the United States to promote our country abroad. I think it's easier for foreigners to relate to a beautiful assortment of U.S. luxury products than tractors, guns, or wheat.

XVI

Hire as I Say,
Not as I Hired!

ONE OF THE MOST DIF-
ficult things for anyone to do, whether hiring a housekeeper or
a general manager, is to conduct the kind of job interview that
will yield the information one needs to know to tell whether
the interviewee is really qualified. The problem is com-
pounded when you are in a hurry to fill a specific position or
when you like the person you are interviewing and want to hire
her or him regardless of capability.

When you are in a hurry to fill a job, you hope "this is the
one" so much that you do all the talking and guide the interview, until the interviewee gives the proper answers. You soon
adopt a tone of, "I know you can do this job" . . . and you end
up selling the interviewee on the role rather than discovering if
it fits.

I've already told of my mistakes in hiring people I liked
without finding their capacity for doing the special job. Well,

in addition to my commandment regarding the danger of hiring friends, I have some others to be added along the way. First, it is not a good idea to hire several persons from the same family group, and certainly not if they are to be working in the same area. For one thing, others will feel there is favoritism. If you have them doing interrelated functions, there can be theft or collusion, which puts a strain on everyone, because, most of the time, fellow workers catch on or begin to suspect it well before there is proof of wrongdoing, and they resent it.

In the early years of our company, I totally ignored a lesson along these lines that I had learned, or thought I learned, at Neiman–Marcus. One Christmas we found we had almost an entire packing group from one family. Soon it was almost as if Neiman–Marcus had taken on an agent when the oldest member of the family began "suggesting" terms to the firm on behalf of himself and his relatives. And, because it was during the busiest season, the company had to adhere to the self-appointed agent's edicts. I remember thinking at the time how dependent one is on packers at Christmas and determining, before I thought of owning my own company, that I would never allow them to be related and working in one section.

A few years later I completely forgot that vow—and, moving on the reverse philosophy that if you liked one worker, then surely the sisters, brothers, and cousins would have the same likable characteristics—I hired a whole company of wonderful, related people. What happened was inevitable. Even within one family the good characteristics aren't always passed along. We ended up with a terrible situation in which one member had been hired as a skilled typist, another had been hired to sweep floors, others to pack . . . yet they all compared wages and decided they were being treated unfairly because the wages were unequal. Events then piled up rapidly: I was informed that working conditions were not satisfactory, that there was a draft by one person's chair, that a table wobbled, that the typist's typewriter wasn't new enough . . . and before I knew what was happening, I was being formally "visited" by the family group and by an employment grievance team from a certain section of Dallas and was informed how unfair I was.

Having been a sociology major in college who studied just such things in detail, and considering myself a generally liberal person, politically, socially, and economically, I was astounded, hurt, then angered at this criticism. To make matters worse, our company was concurrently sued by a family member who worked opening letters—actually, who operated the machine which automatically opened the letters. This person claimed to have been bypassed for promotion when the head of Order Processing moved to another job and the letter-opener was not given the opportunity to become head of Order Processing.

My answer was that it is quite a long distance between opening the envelopes containing the orders and being in charge of the entire section that processes the orders—but that didn't stop the charges from being filed. After two years and thousands of dollars worth of lawyer fees, we were judged innocent and the case was dismissed. What a shame to waste so much time, to have so much mutual uneasiness on something like this. If only I had remembered the lesson I already knew about not hiring members of the same family.

More mistakes? Certainly . . .

In a short course at the Harvard Business School, one of the things I thought I had learned was that it is seldom a good idea for a small business to hire a recent college graduate, especially one from a major business school. This may sound unfair, but in practice business school graduates are too often anxious to change the company entirely based on classroom theory, without having much on-line experience. It isn't so bad with a large firm where there is enough cushion to protect the machinery from error, but it can be dangerous in a smaller concern where every change has to work.

Again, I chose to ignore a piece of information I had paid quite a bit of time and money to acquire, and I decided that I would, indeed, hire bright, fresh-out-of-college young people because they would have their minds less cluttered and could bring invigorating ideas to problem solving. We hired one young man to run Order Processing (he had superb academic qualifications), and within a week the suggestion box was no longer used for suggestions, it was stuffed with complaints—violent complaints. What appeared to be a bright young man with ideas turned out to be another personnel disaster. His biggest achievement was moving the file cabinets from one side of the room to the other (disrupting the flow so they had to be moved again), getting rid of twelve employees who had been with us almost since our beginning, and alienating half the staff in general before he left.

Another young man was hired to be very aggressive and take care of reordering of merchandise, making sure that the people working in that section kept right on top of the reorders. I had asked one of the people from business school to come spend a week analyzing the needs of the reorder section, so this job was specifically outlined. Now this is a case of hoping the person interviewed can match the requirements of the job because we were in a hurry to get it going. We asked all the right questions, and, when you do that, you can only expect to get the "right" answers. This young man lasted about three weeks. His contribution toward an aggressive reorder policy was simply to scrap the previously workable system and install his own cumbersome substitute; again, he almost caused us a breakdown.

Had I supervised his specific performance more carefully, I might have been able to salvage this young man's job with us, but it was at the very busiest time of the year, and, since we had fully outlined job responsibility, I felt he could handle it—but he couldn't. I should have asked more questions the answers to which weren't from the textbook, but I was in a hurry, and he was so enthusiastic and assured—so perfect for the job.

My next major mistake in hiring (I warned you there were plenty more) came when I signed up an expert without really being certain his expertise was needed by our company. We determined, after a very difficult time with the computer during Christmas, that we must have on staff a very knowledgeable computer expert, even though it might be costly. We had had so many problems during our first year with the computer that we were desperate for a solution. For a not-so-brief period the computer sent two packages on each order form, but we didn't know it because there was nothing to indicate what the computer was doing. Lucky for us, some of the customers began calling, "Hey, you've sent me two nightgowns (or sets of dishes or Cartier watches) and I just ordered one." The computer lost the names, and we had to write hundreds of rather pitiful letters begging, "If you've received two of whatever you ordered will you please send one back?" Luckily our customers proved to be honest and did so—at least, the ones we were able to contact.

What we didn't realize, in our computer-bred panic, was that we needed a worker, a nuts-and-bolts man, and not a superexec who was familiar only with machines capable of running a billion-dollar corporation. We interviewed four or five experts and even though we liked one or two others, we finally decided, in a burst of management awareness and enthusiasm, to hire the top of the line, the most experienced and the most expensive.

He arrived talking all sorts of computerese and immediately ordered the largest machine being manufactured and put our name on the list for an even larger one as yet unmade. (I went through two years praying the thing wouldn't be delivered by mistake, since we didn't have room for it then or now.) Meanwhile, our expert drew up table upon table of organization, listing assistant after assistant, programmer following programmer. Had we fulfilled his dreams of glory we would presently be mostly in the computer business and only partly in the mail-order business.

Fortunately for us, we had gone so high up the tree to gather our top banana that he was really only biding time with us, and, at the first opportunity of a vice-presidency and a slightly higher salary (*slightly*, because he was already getting tops in his line), he quickly departed. He later announced he was ready to come back to us, for the right title and an even higher salary, but I humbly deferred until, perhaps, we hit a billion-dollar plateau.

Yet another mistake, opposite in a way from the "top banana" mistake, is to hire a person with no specific talent only because you hope that person's intelligence can be put to use someplace in your organization. We did a lot of that in the early days, because we didn't have nearly so well-defined an organization as we later developed. In fact, you might say that in our very beginning days we were *all* in the category of hopeful talent. But the hiring mistake I'm talking about comes well after that. It comes when you think you have things down so smoothly that you can afford to gamble or experiment. There were several employees who started with us in a kind of searching-out role and progressed along the way, and some of them left feeling very disappointed with the company for having mistreated them in one way or another.

One example was a young man who started working for me almost on the first day I opened the front door. He did not have a college degree and had little working experience, but, because of his intelligence and his great personal charm and willingness, he gradually worked his way through the company, from floor sweeper to section head of almost every one of our work functions. He wasn't always well-suited to every job function, but he really was intelligent, and, because of my general fondness for him, we worked him through various jobs until he hit one, buying, which he did very well. Eventually we found an analytical area (a very sensitive position, by the way) at which he excelled.

It was at this point, I suppose, that we failed him, for, in attempting to broaden his horizon as much as possible—by exposing him to the outside world through buying trips and attendance at trade conventions—he soon became convinced that his work was worth much more than we were paying him, and he left us to join a new competing mail-order firm. Maybe this shouldn't go down as a hiring mistake or as a failure to predict character, because hiring this young man worked out well. Our failure was in not developing more challenges for him and therefore preserving his loyalties to us.

Another case somewhat similar would be that of the fifty-year-old housewife who came to work for us when her children went off to college. Again, we represented her first job. She did well, working her way from clipping off the mailing labels on returned catalogues to taking charge of renting our lists to other firms and arranging list rentals for us. She parlayed her personality and our speedy growth into a position as spokesperson for Horchow in the important field of buying and selling names. But, before we knew it, the organization was being interpreted by her to the outside world at large, not just to the list brokers. And even though I made many pronouncements about the rules and conditions under which I would, or would not, rent our lists, she increasingly exerted her own power, or sense of power, to misinterpret our ground rules, and eventually I had to dismiss her.

This very capable woman was the type of person who, when reviewed on the basis of a mistake, or in an area where she was not pleasing me, would agree completely, promising to correct deficiencies and do much better in the future. This would involve such simple things as talking too long on the phone when transacting the simplest yes-or-no business (the complaints were coming from the other end of the line more than from our end). She would be all right for a couple of weeks, then would revert to her old habits. I would not have let her go for this alone, but she worked the same way in a variety of other areas.

In each of the latter two cases I feel a sense of personal failure at having lost two good people for no valid reason. But what was I to do? The bad feelings on their part came from their having a measurement of their worth to the company that was unrealistic at the time. Each of the departing employees I mentioned felt she or he had saved, or earned, so much money for the firm that we were holding back what amounted to a vast increase in their salaries. For instance, you are a buyer for us and you discover, when all the sales are recorded, that our profit on some particular product you bought may have been as high as $20,000, so you decide you should get half of that amount because you picked the item. Or you increased the size of a rental order from 50,000 to 100,000 names and you should be given cash credit for the fact that the renter was willing to double his order.

Both these attitudes fail to take into account the fact that the person doing the buying, renting, or selling is merely an instrument, representing an organization of great numbers, many of whom do not have a direct role in purchasing or selling but are indispensable to profits. This attitude also fails to give credit to the team aspects of an organization. In effect, it is the organization itself which promotes the item, produces the catalogue, trains the buyer, pays for the merchandise, and supplies the opportunity to exercise the individual's talents and skills.

It's awfully hard to say what someone is worth in the total scheme of things in an organization because no position is independent of or unrelated to the value of any other position. I suppose the person who has to take the most responsibility for failure comes closest to having a unique value. In the Horchow organization, of course, I am that person. However, I do not draw a grand salary—it won't compare to the salaries of many of the executives with whom I do business—and I don't use my salary as a measure of success or of my happiness. I get more enjoyment from being able to work in the manner I desire, doing what I like to do without having to constantly worry about the scrutiny of someone else. The Horchow organization is essentially a plain company. Our offices are efficient, not grand, we generally travel tourist class and have no yachts or company jets, and all the emphasis is on what the customers see and buy and how they are treated. Yet I believe that ours is a happy place of employment. If there is unhappiness, the suggestion boxes are there to be filled—and I do the first reading.

I have a book which dates from when I first started the business. It is titled *When My Ship Comes In,* and Carolyn and I wrote down all the things we could think of that we wanted at that time. They weren't many: a swimming pool and a pool guesthouse, a trip to Italy for our daughters, and some folk art for our home. Later I added a painting of the girls in the pool as one of my wishes, and an addition to the house so I could entertain lots of people—all of which we have now done. Occasionally Carolyn will say to me, or I will say to her, "We'd better get some more things ready for the next ship!"

XVII

Dear Customer:
Let's Overcommunicate

SOMETHING I LIKE about presiding over the Horchow Collection is that our customers regard us so personally. There are those who call in orders or send them by mail, who have an image of Horchow as a cozy little place with three or four sweet ladies taking orders who, as soon as they hang up the phone, run back and take down the order from the shelf, wrap it, and mail it themselves, dusting off their hands and saying, "There!" in a well-pleased tone. I couldn't count the times customers have said to a telephone worker, "Now, didn't you take my last order? Seems to me it was you," or, "You remember me, don't you? . . . I bought one of those darling pink robes you had last Christmas."

The marvelous thing is, it's surprising how often one of the phone operators really does recognize a repeat customer—and with as many as 25,000 orders a week, about 40 percent of them by telephone, that's stacking the odds pretty high. Blanche Liebenson, who was in charge of the telephone-order room, was on hand back when we had just one telephone line; remember, it wasn't very long ago that mail-order business was just what it says: mail order. Horchow turned that around with massive telephone ordering any time a customer wants to call. Blanche has a remarkable ear for voices from every corner of North America. If you called and started telling her about your hometown (our customers frequently pass on local news), you might discover Blanche had already heard your story—even if it only occurred this morning.

But, to preserve this personal relationship as much as possible, to keep Horchow as near a one-to-one business as growth and numbers will permit, takes daily planning. It starts with a roundtable meeting in my office each morning with about eight or nine of the people who keep things running. Everything done at that meeting relates to the question: Are we taking care of the customers? If I'm away, the meeting takes place just the same, and I hear the information by phone.

The first report I look at tells me what the company did yesterday, then I ask, "How is the mail today?" The table looks over the predictions that Helen Mary Thomas, Bob Frame, and Jim Mabry make for the number of orders received for the day, the week, and the catalogue that is currently mailed. They are all broken down with predictions of better, or worse, numbers in all those categories.

At Horchow, we work with eight catalogues at one time, although there may be several items in some books that have either sold out or have stopped selling. After getting predictions, I look at what happened the previous day—how the orders broke down into numbers and dollars—and where we stand in our predictions.

I then get a rough mail count for the morning, because by 9 A.M. the order department has looked at several thousand pieces of mail. We have a post-office box and we know just about what we are going to get from one day to the next. If there isn't much in our box, we knock on the window and ask, "Don't you have some more for Horchow?" and most of the time the postal clerk will go back and find another sack. If he says, "There just isn't any more," we know we'll have to call the Dallas postmaster's office and someone there will say, "Oh, yeah . . . there's some at the bulk-mail center we haven't picked up yet." It's sort of all in the family, and the post-office people know we know what we're supposed to have, so they generally cooperate if we say, "There's got to be some more." During heavy buying seasons the postal service will keep trucks and personnel at our warehouse to handle our packages so that one or two postal processes can be skipped.

There has been a lot of criticism of the U.S. Postal Service, but, I must say, we have gotten acceptable service throughout our years. Of course, we do quite a bit of the work ourselves, keeping zip codes separate and that kind of thing. My main complaint has been the climbing cost of parcel post. It is so high that, like most big shippers, Horchow has been forced, more and more, to use the private delivery services—which aren't always that much better, but are more reasonable. Compared to most other countries, though, the U.S. postal system is excellent.

The biggest piece of paper I look at each day is the computer report which tells me how much merchandise we got in, how much we have on hand, what is out-of-stock, how we are coming in sales, and whether the order backlog has built up, which isn't desirable, because we've got the customer's money but we haven't shipped the order, and he's going to be mad at us. By law, if we don't ship an order within twenty-one days of the amount of time stated in the catalogue, we have to get the customer's written permission to hold the order, so we are very careful.

If something has to be monogrammed or handmade, we state a longer time for delivery, but, if an item has no stated delivery time, we have twenty-one days to get it to you. If there is an unexpected delay, we always ask if the customer wants the item badly enough to wait, even if the waiting period is several weeks. We only give up when you tell us to give up, unless, of course, the item isn't any longer obtainable.

We try to ship immediately, but, if our suppliers haven't delivered to us, we're stuck. With suppliers worldwide, we've heard every imaginable excuse for not delivering. These are actual replies to our frantic queries of, "What has happened to our shipment?"

- The ship sank . . . or missed the Port of Houston . . . or sailed with the cargo still on the dock.
- The air shipment got lost in New York . . . or there was no space for it on the plane.
- The factory closed for vacation . . . or burned down.
- The package fell off the truck.
- The train derailed.
- The rains came and nothing would dry.
- The village was wiped out by fire (or monsoon).
- The woman had a baby—or his wife had a baby and he didn't come to work.
- The weavers (potters, dyers, etc.) joined the Revolution.
- The stock boy thought it had been shipped but it hadn't.
- The supplier forgot to order more, or couldn't get enough raw material to fill the order.
- The shipment was delayed on the dock by a shipping strike.
- The shipment is being held up by customs.
- The shipment was lost in the manufacturer's computer.
- We sold the order to somebody else.

These may sound amusing in the retelling, but they're not funny when they keep us from getting orders to our customers on time.

International origins can cause peculiar headaches. In our spring catalogue of 1978, we offered a hurricane lamp that could be stuck in the ground or set on a table. The glass chimney was made in Italy and brought into Houston, where the candle was made. A wicker shield which went around the chimney came from the Philippines. A small wooden piece which allowed the lamp to sit upright on the table was from Thailand. It could have been produced any place but it happened to come from Thailand where the monsoon season begins in April.

We found ourselves getting three thousand more orders for the hurricane lamp than we ever dreamed we'd get. We used up all the reserve stock we'd bought and all the importer's stock, but we still had several hundred orders to go. The process of gathering the parts began and that was when we found out about the monsoon season in Thailand, when everything goes under water, and that we could get no more little round wooden things for a while.

We wrote all the customers waiting for hurricane lamps to say, "It's going to be August and summer will be nearly over, and you're probably not going to want the lamps so we will send your money back unless you tell us to hold it." Amazingly, most customers still wanted the lamps. In some cases we shipped everything but the little wooden piece and sent a $5 rebate. That was quite a bit more than the wooden piece was worth, and a good many customers probably hadn't planned to use the lamps on the table anyway, but my philosophy is, if you have to do something you wish you didn't have to do, extend yourself. The extra dollar you extend yourself will come back to you many times over in word-of-mouth reputation. This was the case with the lamps. Customers wrote us such nice things as, "Thanks for the bargain. The lamp only cost $16 to begin with and the little wooden piece couldn't have been worth nearly one-third that amount." Some even protested: "It's still possible to use it on a table, it just wobbles." But the greatest number of replies said, in effect, "That was nice of you," and all those customers will tell the story when anyone mentions hurricane lamps . . . or Horchow.

The shipping report (getting back to my daily reading), which gives the average order in terms of number of items ordered and amount of dollars, tell us whether the customers like the catalogue, or if they like it enough to be spending a bit more than ordinary. Of course, if the average order is lower, it's saying to us, "You people missed something, because we're only spending $34 when it would have been just as easy to spend $40 as we've been doing before." If we see that the average order is going to remain below our projections (and it only takes a week or so to tell), then we begin to look at the catalogue and see what we've done wrong.

There are many unknown reasons why the customers might buy more—reasons outside the scope of our predictions—so we can't always assume that we know what caused the sales bulge. Take those hurricane lamps. There was nothing we could point to and say, "This created sales."

But if the lamps hadn't sold to expectations, we would have had to start finding answers, because the fault would have been ours. You can't drop failure the way you can success. You can be happy with success, and, if you did everything the way you thought you should and you succeeded, then you can simply stick with the game plan and do it again in the next catalogue. That's one secret of retailing: Dissect failures *afterward* and compose success *before*.

We have regular "postmortems" of the catalogues every week to see precisely where we stand with each book that is still producing orders. If sales projections indicate it, we have to start reordering almost from the day the first catalogue gets into the customer's hands. Let's take a catalogue we mailed

May 1, from which we expect 100,000 orders in thirty-two weeks, which is how long we keep track of each book. From experience, we know we will have approximately 50 percent of our orders in the first four weeks after the first order comes back. From the receipt of the first one hundred orders, we say, "The clock is running." If we're going to get our 100,000 orders in thirty-two weeks, we ought to have 50,000 orders in the four weeks after the clock has started. (Then it takes forever to wind down, and, toward the end of the thirty-two-week cycle we are getting one hundred or fewer orders per week.)

But the problem is that we couldn't possibly buy enough of each item in each book to sell at the rate of 100,000 total orders, or for every item to sell at that ratio. Customers don't buy proportionately, and we don't know if they will buy more of *this* or of *that*, so in the beginning we buy what we consider will be an average amount of an average seller in every item. If it's something we have a hunch is going to be a good seller, or if it's something that is going to be hard to get future deliveries on (like an import), we look into the crystal ball and gamble. The computer can't help us *before* something is offered, and all it can tell us after orders start coming in is, "If it keeps up at this rate, you'll sell this amount of goods by this point in time."

Now you can immediately envision a bunch of people sitting around a table in a darkened room with turbans on their heads and a glass ball in their midst. That's the way we have to operate lots of times—on at least 20 percent of the items, even in our marvelous computer age. We laugh a lot in those meetings. I say, "What do you think?" and everybody looks at the buyer, or Dee Foley, an experienced assistant, and those two will look at Tom Holzfeind, my assistant, who is head of forecasting, and Tom will look around at me, and I'll say, "I don't know."

We have to do a lot of guessing. There is still much of the

human element involved. For instance, if one person orders ten or fifteen of an item the very first thing, to give as graduation gifts, it will distort those very early totals and make it appear that the demand is going to be greater than later facts support. We've had individuals order as many as fifty of an item, early on, and, unless we keep in mind that this is only one order, it can mislead the computer and us. On the other hand, we can't disregard those early projections, because, more often than not, they will give fair warning of an avalanche.

My first secretary was named Mary. To save everybody the trouble of walking back to the Receiving Department every morning, I told the people on the receiving dock to keep an informal list of everything they got in and give it to Mary. Mary's been gone since 1973, but we still get "Mary's List" every morning. It's very important, because all the people at the planning session need to know what has arrived. The warehouse manager finds out how many out-of-stock items have come in, the packing manager may need more packers, personnel starts figuring if we need more keypunch operators from the available worker files we keep.

Mary's List alerts the creative departments, too. The Art Department wants to see a new item for the catalogue, the copywriters may want to take a look, and the buyers must see things before we can accept the shipment, because they must make sure it's what we ordered four, six, or a dozen months ago. When a shipment arrives, the receiving department opens a box at random and takes out one or two of the items and sends them to the buyer who made the purchase to be sure it's what was bought.

The buyer often has to refresh his or her memory, so the purchase order is included. If the buyer is supposed to be looking at children's Bible story records, it can't be Benny Goodman or Bing Crosby instead. In addition, the buyer establishes any special instructions for the packers. For example, a particular candleholder must be packed in sets of two with candles, because we advertised "two glass horses and two red candles." The packers won't know this unless these instructions stipulate it. This usually doesn't take more than a minute, but woe unto us if we fail to do it, or if some tiny detail is overlooked.

When a catalogue is just about ready to go out in the mail (they are mailed from the printer), we ask all the people in the order department and the telephone room to bring lunches, and we set up tables with one of every item, from dessert sets to music boxes, and racks with all the clothing, and we have our "Show & Tell." The workers ask all the questions they need to know ("What's that tune on the music box?") and get to handle all the items. They try on clothing to see how it fits, and they try to think of everything the man or woman on the telephone will ask: Is it colorfast? Does it run large or small? Will it fit petite or extra large if it's a one-size-fits-all garment?

These "Show & Tell" sessions are a lot of fun and create lots of gaiety among those who will be taking the orders. A few of the items we offer are rather expensive (furs, diamonds, designer clothes) and draw long, appreciative whistles or covetous looks and caresses. Some young mechanic's wife, for instance, may pose before a mirror with a rare necklace on, dreaming of the day in the future when she can own something so beautiful . . . or an older woman may wrap herself in a fur stole and remember times when she swept into a crowded room, turning every head in her direction. And there will be lines of pretty girls holding up gaily colored dresses and skirts or blouses and aprons, almost like a chorus line doing a dance routine in a swirl of materials.

On a few such occasions our order department people have predicted a dismal sale for some piece, or have seen indications we would have trouble with returns—and they have been remarkably accurate with their forecasts.

We get a printout every morning of orders for $75 and over, not because we want to see who spends the most money but because we want to make sure there wasn't an error in listing—a wrong quantity entered, perhaps, that would cause the order to jump past the average. One time somebody entered one hundred of a $100 item and some of us around the meeting table exclaimed, "Just look how many orders are on that," but we studied the printout, sent for the original written order, and discovered it was an error—one too many zeroes.

On the other hand, the "over-$75" printout is lots of fun, because most times celebrities emerge, or there are customers who *have* spent a lot of money and the zeroes are *correct.* We wouldn't be human, would we, if we weren't curious? We get some famous name every day on the over-$75 list, and who knows how many call in under-$75 orders? We don't keep a list, but some names stand out. Economic royalty or royalty by blood, they all seem to like mail-order shopping. I mentioned Princess Grace of Monaco, and we have done business with Charles Bronson, Paul Anka, Barbra Streisand, Happy Rockefeller, and the late John Wayne (who sent pictures to the people who took his order). Add to that list Gloria Steinem, Dinah Shore, Christina Ford, Sharon Percy Rockefeller, Robert Redford, Lucille Ball, Liza Minelli, the late Hubert Humphrey, several Kennedys, du Ponts, and Rothschilds ... and just about every well-known television performer.

But we don't really value a star's order more than another customer's, although it is always a thrill for someone in the phone room suddenly to hear a familiar voice speaking right to her. I am told that, by and large, celebrities are a very reasonable group from whom to take orders. My daughter Regen worked in the phone room during a school holiday and got an order from Natalie Cole, and Regen said it was just like meeting her in person. I met a famous movie star at a New York party, and, when she heard my name, she asked if I happened to be the Horchow of the Horchow Collection. I said I was, and she told me about what good treatment she had received from the Horchow telephone crew.

"Sure," I said, "but let's be realistic. You're a star. They're polite to everyone who calls, but they know your name."

"Ah, but that's not the case," she said. "I call the order in and use my married name. They don't know who that is."

Everywhere I go I hear about our phone operators, the front line of our organization. In lots of people's minds they are the Horchow Collection *and* Roger Horchow, even though I write little notes and letters to the customers in most of the catalogues.

This inclination to think "Roger Horchow" is made up is a natural enough response on the part of the American consumers who, for years and years, have read things supposedly written by "Betty Crocker" or other trademark characters used by certain corporations. But a small part of this doubtful approach to me is my own fault. In 1971, when I began the Kenton Collection catalogue, I signed letters in the catalogue "Silas Kenton," and I answered business letters under the same name. Carolyn answered complaint letters under the name "Abigail Kenton," and before long we were getting fan letters from all sorts of people. One woman wrote Silas Kenton, "To have a business letter answered by a real person, not a computer, is pure music—even poetry."

Abigail Kenton developed her own style: "Silas tells me you're terribly upset about not receiving that Wyeth plate yet. I cross my heart, though, that you'll get it in plenty of time. . . ."

Eugenia Sheppard, in her "Inside Fashion" newspaper column, described Silas Kenton as, "pure cornball . . . youngish, honest-looking, and talks with a corny Texas drawl," although she knew very well "Silas" was from Ohio!

"His New York office that he visits once a month is decorated with a red, white, and blue poster of his favorite hero, George Washington," she continued, "and Silas is looking for a portrait of his grandfather to go with it. The first Silas Kenton made a mint in the late 19th century but died in despair on Black Monday in 1929. Though the elder Silas's original portrait was lost in the family crash, Silas figures he can find one somewhere that's enough like it to keep him in an upright, all-American mood."

We carried the Kenton family tree right through the organization. Morgan Kenton, Silas's alleged older brother, was named for the trust company, and he had the dirty job of writing the last stern note to delinquent bill payers. After two formal notices, Morgan Kenton's letter mentioned The Law . . . but in the friendliest, down-home way possible. Silas Kenton also described how he got ideas for his catalogue: "I just sat down and tried to think what Uncle Ebenezer and Aunt Sally would like for Christmas, and it turned out right."

At the tail end of her column, Eugenia wrote, "Of course, there are those who don't believe there is such a person as Silas Kenton. They think he's an old school chum with an advertising background, married to a girl named Carolyn, whose picture appears in a silver-gift frame in the Kenton Christmas catalogue. Some people are just born skeptical about anything that's good and corny, aren't they?"

I'll admit, I miss Silas Kenton. I like the idea of him and Abigail and Morgan (stern though he was) and Uncle Ebenezer and Aunt Sally, and the personal letters from Silas and Abigail. Someday I may even see if it is possible to resurrect Silas and Abigail, although if enough people think "Roger

Horchow" is a manufactured name I guess my job now is to convince them he is alive and well and living in Dallas.

But the Silas Kenton theme, with its personal overtones, is my idea of an ideal approach to doing business. I do not like people to think I am a machine or that my company is run by a machine—although it would be impossible to run it without a computer. I like the thought, no matter what the business, that somewhere at the top there is a flesh-and-blood person to whom I can take a problem and my complaints—and I know my customers do, too.

Our Customer Service department is, by our standards, the heart of our operation. The daily report from Customer Service is like the doctor's chart at the foot of the patient's bed (or at the nurses' station, if you think the other is too old-fashioned.) It gives me the temperature, pulse rate, respiration count, blood analysis—everything I want to know about our daily business health; in other words, what the customers are saying (and thinking) about our service.

I get a breakdown of every type letter that comes in. Jan Coleman, in Customer Service, has figured out that there are only twenty reasons someone writes us a letter, and most of them have to do with problems over which we have no control. First, as I mentioned, there is the Wismo, or one of its variations: Where is my refund? Where is my check? Then there are the routine reports: It arrived broken, it's the wrong size, I want to return this, what am I going to do with this? And finally, the two broad categories: I love you and I hate you.

I read all the letters that say, literally or figuratively, "I hate you." They come to me in a basket marked "CRITICAL" and I see everyone of them because they tell me what's wrong with some part of our organization, even when they attack us for something that isn't really our fault. If someone is so moved as to write a letter and tell me where she, or he, thinks we have failed, then that's very helpful. Even if we didn't fail, the customer thinks we did, so perhaps there is room for improvement or a change of procedure.

And the legitimate complaints are a great help. When I get one, I look around and see how to correct things—and, in many cases, I'd never have known if a customer hadn't told me. If it's some procedural error, we obviously thought it was a good idea before; if it's not now working, the customers will probably be the first to tell us. We've changed a number of procedures—in fact, most of them—because the customers pointed out flaws to us.

As a customer (speaking now as a consumer, not the head of a business), I always write letters to people who fail to live up to my expectations and their own advertising, because that's what I would like people to do to me. Quite a few of you may think that isn't very nice, and a lot of businesses get downright irate over the least flaw you bring to their attention, but my philosophy is, if it means that much to someone—so that he will write a letter or call and lecture me—then I'd better pay attention, because that one letter or call may represent a hundred unmailed complaints.

I tell my Customer Service persons, "Overcommunicate with the customer." We're better off sending information they don't want to know than keeping back something that will perhaps change their plans. We'd rather a customer be mad at us because of something we *had* to tell him than be mad because of something we *failed* to tell him.

Part of our "overcommunication" is directed by the computer. It rejects bad credit orders and automatically notifies customers of delays—that kind of thing. It does a good job, and is absolutely necessary, but it makes me feel bad. The first ten catalogues I sent out, in Kenton days, had a special message from me: "We're a new company, we care about you, the customer, and you'll never be answered by a computer."

That was true, and possible, in the days when we numbered our customers by the thousands, not hundreds of thousands. Now we must rely on the computer for certain responses, especially responses to problems the computer can answer more quickly than human me. But, in truth, a customer is not answered *by* the computer, even today, because a human reads every letter. The return message is often initiated by the computer, but the message is composed by a human being—so I feel I'm still living up to the spirit of my pledge.

Finally, in our daily morning meeting, we go around the table for the last time asking for problems. That usually brings up little things like a warning from Kitty Lane, head of Customer Service, "You know, we've been having a problem with that gray dress. It's beginning to come back pretty heavily." This alerts us to the fact that we need to talk to the buyer, which, in turn, may cause us to go out and buy dressmaker's dummies so we can try every shipment from that manufacturer that comes in—put a dress of each size on the dummy to see if every size is right. We buy an initial cutting of a dress and it may fit a certain way that's different from the usual size—or, in other cases, the manufacturer has been known to mislabel.

With this odds-and-ends period concluded (though sometimes it can run longer than the rest of the meeting combined), the morning gathering ends. Then, except for emergencies, I am not apt to see anybody who was at the meeting for the rest of the day. They're all busy within their sections, making their own decisions, and, if anything arises that causes them to have to contact me, it will be unusual. My office is always open and I am always available, but, frankly, at that point in the day I suppose I could leave, as far as running the business is concerned.

XVIII

More Secrets?
You're Entitled

Every week or so someone will come calling with a scheme. Sometimes we are asked to invest in a new machine that will do some wonderful thing, or, on other occasions, we are offered an advanced mechanism for some machine we are already using. But the most frequently presented scheme is that of someone, or some firm, with an idea they feel certain would make me rich—if we would only put our catalogue in *their* store, or if I would only help them do *their* catalogue.

In most cases of new machinery, if a machine really has been developed that will increase our efficiency, we have to look closely, because few machine makers can turn out something which precisely fits our problem. We see a new machine that performs some function and we say, "That might work for us this way or that, but not exactly the way it was designed to work." As for business schemes, a lot of them are probably good, but such schemes overlook the fact that I am wrestling with my own scheme, trying to make it work right before I can take on someone else's—and, as for getting rich, I'm not dedicated to that goal.

A lot of people who come to see me really just want information. This can lead to awkward interludes. I don't mind answering questions, but information is as important a part of our operation as is the inventory. Even the simplest piece of information about the mail-order business has been gained at a high cost. None of it is simple, yet every day someone approaches me as if information were a public commodity like the weather forecast. It can be terribly difficult to tell somebody that what they're asking is a trade secret or is none of their business. You keep hoping he will catch on and quit asking. But I don't let discomfort in the face of persistence cause me to give out facts and research findings people have no right to ask for. As I said before, I'm flexible, but not fragile. Sometimes I simply inform questioners I'll consult with them for whatever fee consultants in my field get. Put that way, it usually stops the advance.

One of the reasons I'm writing this book is to answer questions about Horchow and the mail-order business. I am telling a great many secrets in the process, but I think that if someone is willing to buy a book to learn the secrets, that puts it in a better light. When you finish reading this book, you will know all of the secrets of mail order that I am going to tell.

Horchow is a highly visible company with thousands of calls and letters coming every day, so we never know who or what may be behind any particular contact. It might be an inquiry motivated by curiosity or it might be from someone in competition. The worst thing that happens—and it comes under the heading of chutzpah rather than ethics, I suppose—is that other retailers will call up, in the guise of customers, and ask where something came from or from whom we bought it. Or they pretend, when we're out of stock or a catalogue is finished, that they just want to buy something on their own and we shouldn't care if we tell them. (Incidentally, we don't pull these tricks on stores or other catalogues.)

My feeling on this matter is that we've spent thousands of dollars, plus energy and shoe leather, looking for these goods. It's no big secret that if someone else went to the same place he could find them, but just where that place is is our business. It will be soon enough, I've learned from sad experience, that the source itself will be sending out trade brochures saying, "As seen in the Horchow Collection catalogue."

Sometimes the global nature of modern manufacturing creates amusing sidelights. A customer in Hong Kong orders an electronic gadget from us, then gets our letter saying we are temporarily out of stock but that the manufacturer is shipping a new order and can the customer wait three weeks? The customer writes back that three weeks is okay, and the same day that her letter leaves Hong Kong coming to us, the new shipment of electronics also leaves the manufacturer, coming to us—from within two blocks of where the customer lives. We receive the electronic shipment and immediately dispatch to our customer in Hong Kong whatever piece was ordered, sending it back two blocks from where it started its 10,000-mile journey.

Almost every day several persons from outside the mail-order industry want to see me, and I like to have my schedule relaxed enough so that they can stay as long as they think they need to. Some of them are acquaintances interested in working for the company, others are trying to interest me in projects of one kind or another, some worthwhile, others pure fantasy. And if I am to be interviewed by some media reporter, I like to have plenty of time so that I can be sure I am being understood.

I can put up with anybody any time if they tell me the truth, no matter how bad it is. We try to pass this along to our customers: We're going to tell you the truth without hedging. So I get really angry when a supplier tells me, "Oh, I meant to call you back but something happened," when I have a thousand customers waiting for his shipment. I get into the act when my buyers have failed and the reorder department has failed. My buyers laugh and say I enjoy those confrontations, and I guess I do, because when I have them dead to rights, I don't mind telling them so. If someone says, "I'll be there tomorrow between 9 and 12 A.M.," and I'm still waiting at 3 P.M., I get furious. I'm very tolerant of reasonable excuses, but not lies to cover up failings. If a repair person calls and says, "Sorry, I can't make it by noon," or calls back and says, "I still can't make it, maybe you'd better get someone else," I can understand.

I also get furious at people who seem to think I was born yesterday. People who say, for instance, "Oh, yes, you have an exclusive on this," then it appears in somebody else's catalogue at exactly the same time as ours. Also, you'd think if a supplier has an order for $10,000 worth of merchandise, and doesn't get our money until he ships to us, he'd want to get it out as quickly as possible. But even in recessions there is so much business, and people have so much, there isn't enough economic pressure to keep sellers alert, or even interested. The sound man who promised to install my stereo system last week finally says he'll get to it Monday, then Wednesday, now it's Friday. He has a captive audience, more work than he can handle anyhow. He's the best, who else can you go to?

Or the swimming pool. Does anyone in the United States have a satisfactory pool-service company? The boy who is supposed to clean the pool once a week (as per contract) has something else to do that day—he's going to a ballgame or someone suddenly says, "Let's go to Galveston. . . ." Oh, he'll get around to it sooner or later, but, meantime, the pool is dirty.

It's the worst thing happening in this country, and it alarms me because it's not just a teen-ager who decides to take off with friends, or a one-man expert who has no competition. It can be just as bad among the biggest corporations in the world. I feel so powerless, as do most passengers, when I have an unhappy experience on one airline, switch to another, and have the same unhappy experience there. You don't have any other choice.

And when you write a letter of protest, even if it happens to be read by some higher official, you find he is at the mercy of somebody else—some intermediate supervisor or manager, even somebody else's secretary—and no matter what company advertising promises, nothing's going to change. I wrote a letter once to the head of a huge grocery store chain, telling him I wished his stores would keep a certain kind of dry cereal in stock. He wrote back and assured me the chain had not dropped that brand of cereal and that it would be available from now on, that running out of it had been purely an oversight, and blah, blah, blah. Well, the cereal didn't show up again on the shelves of the store where I shopped, and I finally asked a stockboy on the cereal aisle—hadn't Mr. B, the boss, notified them to keep it in stock? The boy shrugged. Nobody'd said nothin' to him about orderin' it. It never reappeared.

I think I am speaking for a huge segment of American buyers when I say we are the daily victims of indifference and forgotten promises. The words "guaranteed" or "warranted" are virtually meaningless, not always because a manufacturer is trying to cheat but because no one along the line of distribution and service will assume responsibility. American businessmen are fond of that rough-and-ready motto, "The buck stops here." But sometimes the consumer has a hard time finding out just where "here" is. Too many firms let their advertising and public relations departments make public policy for them, then run and hide when consumers try to make them live up to their ads and press releases. I simply will not operate a company that way, and, if I can penetrate the industrial iron curtain, I won't let others get away with operating that way.

Sometimes my Customer Service people feel put upon, I know, but there has to be some place in the Horchow operation where the complaint can always be heard and acted on. I have explained to them, "I realize you poor folks are at the end of the telephone and are opening the mail that brings in those complaints, and you didn't do anything wrong. You sit here doing your work every day, while someone else in the organization, or some manufacturer, is the reason for the complaint. See how important you are?"

We are all powerless in some frustrating situations, but, on the other hand, sometimes, when we finally get to the source, it doesn't help. If you threaten to drop out, the supplier will just sell to someone else, or the service will move down the list to the next customer. Again, using the swimming pool as example: Dallas has an enormous number of residential pools because of the long hot spring, summer, and fall season, so a swimming pool in Dallas is not necessarily a sign of affluence. But, with all these thousands of pools, satisfactory maintenance and repair service is hard to find.

We had the same pool-service company for three years, but gradually I realized I was throwing money away. We got used to having a dirty pool when we planned a pool party—the day after the pool service was supposed to have cleaned it up. And, invariably, after a certain day of the week the pool itself overflowed because someone had forgotten to close a valve properly. I warned the maintenance firm twice that if service wasn't satisfactory, I would have to cancel. The woman who took my call said, "I sure understand and I wouldn't blame you."

Well, it all happened again, so one Monday morning I

called and told them to cancel my service at the end of the month.

The woman said, "All right."

I said, "I've been your customer for three years. Don't you even want to know why you're losing a customer?"

She said, "Well, you have the right to cancel."

And I said, "In my business, if the customer is kind enough to call and say, 'Don't mail me the Horchow catalogue anymore,' I'd be curious as to what led to it. . . . I'd think that even though you may not need my business you might just be curious that maybe somebody did something."

She said, "No."

And I said, "Okay," and hung up.

So, they lost nothing, the way they look at it. Just add another name to their service list and drop the old one. True, they've lost a guaranteed profit, a customer they won't have to advertise for or solicit, yet they don't care.

This is the major problem today with American business: They don't care. The pool service doesn't care, the sound system man doesn't care ("Got more business now than I can handle"), the airlines don't care, because their planes are filled. So the homeowners, buyers, and plane riders are powerless, and I'm very frustrated. All I can do, as Roger Horchow of the Horchow Collection, is say (and prove) to my customers, "I care."

I mentioned advertising setting the public policy for some firms, and that only makes it doubly frustrating, because, when you go to the store or the ticket counter and have in your mind all the delightful things the ads have assured you will happen, it's twice as bad when it turns out you get the same old indifferent handling or the same erratic products and servicing. So many large corporations are now "product" corporations. Their entire *raison d'etre* is based on their advertising programs that urge "Buy from us . . ." or "Use us and get the red carpet treatment . . . ," but they know you will go to the store, call for reservations, get on the plane anyway; they don't care.

So I hesitate to advertise the fact that "we care." I just do it. Our advertising money is spent on little magazine ads which say, "Would you like our catalogue? We'd love to send it to you." Those are the only ads we use (except some local ads telling of special bargains in our Finale stores). We really do care, but we don't have to advertise to prove it.

There's a mystique about our organization to the effect that, "It's very special to get the Horchow Collection catalogue." I don't mind the mystique, but I have had a problem with it. Even close friends have come to believe it. Friends will write and say, "My neighbor gets your catalogue and she's not rich . . . what do I have to do to get it?" Or our catalogue request department hears about anxious callers like the woman from Miami who was very angry, telling us, "The Smiths didn't send in for your catalogue until a week after I did, why'd you send it to them first? You think they're better off than I am?" And we get a surprising number of calls from relatives warning us of other relatives: "Don't put them on your mailing list because even if we have the same name, they're poor." (However, sometimes this is done by a well-meaning parent, discussing a new son-in-law or a child's marriage.)

I have really been surprised by the people who seem to think there is some mysterious waiting list for receiving our catalogue. A friend, visiting in Dallas, once said to me, "My sister in Houston is always borrowing my catalogue . . . she'd just *love* to get on your list." Now I happen to remember the sister from the time I lived in Houston, so I felt free to give a little lecture. "John," I said, "we advertise every week in *Vogue, The New Yorker, Better Homes & Gardens, Town & Coun-*

try, or *New York* ... doesn't she get *any* of those? Are we wasting our money?"

But, the problem is, a great many people don't focus on that. My mother will tell me, during a Sunday phone call, about the people she saw this week who would just *love* to get the catalogue, and I'll say, "Mother ... is it because your friends don't read those ads? Just tell them how easy it is to get on the mailing list if they read the ads." Many people who know about the Horchow Collection assume they already know everything our ads say, so the information doesn't soak in.

Frankly, some people within the industry criticize us for not advertising items. We don't know if we're right or wrong, from an economic standpoint, we're just pragmatic about it. We did item-for-item advertising in our earlier magazine blitz, and, although the program was a disaster, that didn't necessarily mean everything we spotlighted was a disaster. Some mail-order firms alternate between advertising only the catalogue and advertising a special product from the catalogue. In most cases their catalogues are more specialized than ours so their image is fixed: When I think of L. L. Bean, for instance, I immediately think of outdoor clothing and camping.

We face a more difficult image problem. We're a luxury catalogue, but, at the same time, we pay close attention to usefulness and style. We would like to have a unified image, and maybe, in another half-dozen years, "Horchow" will conjure up a way of life—but I'm depending on our customers to give the image to us, not just our advertising department.

XIX

Hello There Brookline, Minnetonka, and Sterling Heights

WHEN WE STARTED
the Kenton Collection, we had only one line for telephone
orders. The typical catalogue experience, up to that time, had
been that the vast majority of orders came by mail. Most catalogues were issued by stores and it was felt that phone orders
should go directly to the various departments. On the other
hand, few of the strictly mail-order companies offered phone-
order facilities, and certainly not for free, unless you happen to
live in the town where they were located. Of course, I take a
lot of pride in reminding everyone that the Kenton–Horchow
catalogue was the first general luxury catalogue, broadly distributed, that was not either tied to a retail store or highly
specialized.

Within a few weeks of issuing our first catalogue we had to expand our telephone-order department to three lines, then six. Now we have twenty or more lines with 24-hour-a-day, every-day-in-the-year (yes, even on Christmas) order service, toll free. We also pioneered the 800 numbers for ordering toll free from throughout the continental United States.

Our telephone staff is highly trained, not only to answer questions about catalogue merchandise but to make certain the order is exact on the part of both giver and taker. The phone job is fun, but it is very hard work. I am told by the telephone operators that the time passes quickly ("Zip, and your shift is over"), but they are exhausted when they get off. Some people seem to take to phone work naturally, others last only a few days. Generally speaking, younger women handle the job best—although men are often customer favorites because they are unusual in this type work. There are three main requirements for the job: Order takers must speak distinctly, they must be able to understand all sorts of accents and inflections (because we hear virtually every accent found in the United States and Canada), and they must write legibly when writing in a hurry.

The telephones never stop ringing. If you walk into the Horchow phone room at 10 P.M., 3 A.M., or high noon you will find at least one line bright with a call. And from 10 A.M. to 4 P.M. (Dallas time) every light on the board is lit—which explains why the Horchow order phone sometimes has to ring ten or twelve rings when you call in an order during that period. During the day we never have fewer than twenty-four stations open.

The mail–phone ratio of orders ran about 90–10 the first year we mailed catalogues, then dropped (or changed) to 80–20 for another year, and, after that, telephone orders grew sensationally. For instance, in 1972 we got 4,000 telephone orders, but by 1975 this had grown to 61,000 and by 1977 it had become 135,000. By 1979 the mail–phone ratio was something like 60–40 with phone orders climbing. Telephone orders have a higher initial cost, but this tends to average down as the orders are taken, filled, and paid for. In the first place, phone orders are generally more satisfactory because we can give more information right there at the point of contact; there's less chance for misunderstanding. If some item is temporarily out of stock, or unavailable in a size or color, a replacement can be ordered. In brief, by the time a telephone order is completed, it is an accomplished fact with few possibilities of a return or dissatisfaction. We, of course, like to *know* that the customer has received his or her catalogue and we like the quick response phone orders give. I am sure that telephone ordering will continue to increase, particularly as postage goes up and people become more and more skeptical about mail service. With the prevalent use of credit cards, telephone ordering is unquestionably the best way for an operation like ours to proceed. The greater cost can be offset by saving in time, and someday technology will eliminate even the higher cost.

The phone-order takers keep right up to the minute on every listing in past catalogues as well as the status of each item in the new books. By the time a phone-order person has taken a few hundred calls about items in a particular catalogue, she or he knows instinctively what the customer might ask. Misprints are the terror of the catalogue sales business, and, understandably, the most frustrating discovery a customer can face. Fortunately, we have had only a few, and, when they do occur, the phone room is the best remedy for this error.

On minor misprints we absorb the loss—and misprints always seem to lower the price. And, as Kitty Lane says, "It's always a big winner." The misprinted lower price never seems to come on a bad seller; it's always on something that was expected to be a big seller when we chose it. We have had only one misprint slip through on a really costly item. This was a ladies' coat which knowledgeable shoppers should have known was priced too far below the market to be true. It was, in fact, priced well below our cost. Most of the customers who tried to order the coat by telephone and were informed that the catalogue price was misprinted said something like, "Well, I couldn't believe you meant it." But a few, especially those who mailed orders, were extremely unhappy that we would not ship at the misprint price. Had it been a matter of merely losing money we might have swallowed the several-thousand-dollar loss, but the manufacturer (who spotted the misprint as quickly as we did) warned that if we shipped his coat at that figure, he would no longer ship us anything because our price had brought an immediate outcry from everyone else he did business with who claimed he gave us a better price—and he could be put out of business for price concessions. Needless to say, I don't ever want to go through a situation like that again. We lost money, customers, and pride.

Misprints are bound to happen in catalogue production, no matter how carefully the book is proofread. We had a rather serious misprint on a Cartier watch in 1978 when it was discovered that somewhere in the mill a zero had been dropped off the price and it was listed at $110 rather than $1,100. But we found out in time to include an *erratum* slip in the catalogue before a copy had been mailed.

Our phone room is full of suggestions that come from the phone handlers themselves—someone is always coming up with helpful suggestions or useful "no-nos." My favorite is a card, by each telephone set, giving eleven synonyms for the word "okay." We also try to keep vague words like "deal," "thing," "you know," and "Uhh . . ." and current television slang out of our vocabularies. Some of our customers can't seem to believe that the Horchow Collection "way down there in Texas" can keep up with the times, and they suggest fashion tips or trends "that won't get down there for a while." We are all trained to be patient and try not to refer to anyone as being "from up North" or "back East." However, as I have noted before, a good many customers are rather chatty and will ask about the weather, current events, or what the operators think of things that might be happening in the world, or will tell about new grandchildren, daughters getting married, or sometimes even husbands passing on.

I drop in on the phone room from time to time and listen to some of the conversations, not to check up on the phone operators, but to get some useful ideas from the customers themselves. It is a diverse activity, covering the nation with the speed and the scope of a radar scanner. For instance, during one summer morning, within a space of twelve minutes and simply pushing the lighted buttons on one of our twenty-line sets, I heard, in this order, calls from:

Brookline, Massachusetts
Minnetonka, Minnesota
West Palm Beach, Florida
San Diego, California
Franklin, Tennessee
Charlottesville, Virginia
Greensboro, North Carolina
Dearborn, Michigan
Overland, Missouri
New York, New York
Waterloo, Iowa
Norcross, Georgia
Damascus, Maryland
Glastonbury, Connecticut
Sterling Heights, Michigan
Livingston, New Jersey

While listening, I overhear some rather strange orders and requests. A woman wanted to know if we had "anything with sheep on it," and, if we did, was it suitable for a delayed birthday gift. A man asked if he could get two needlepoint slippers, in different sizes, for the left foot only. One of our telephone ladies asked a woman from Denver, taking her order, "What credit card are you using?" A pause, then an indignant, "Mine!"

One of the persons who worked in the phone room for several years swears that a caller, referring to the name Horchow, asked, "Is he Chinese?"

The operator said, "Well, I'm not sure, but I doubt it. Mr. Horchow doesn't look very Chinese."

The caller said, "Oh, I imagine he is . . . Horchow is *such* a Chinese name."

I am told that quite a few callers ask about the name, wanting to know how it's pronounced or what its origins are. When we first went from "Kenton Collection" to "Horchow Collection," several concerned customers asked if we didn't think a name like that would hurt business.

Every Christmas season we have a few celebrants, or over-celebrants, who call wanting to play Santa Claus without a credit card, but, when you consider that we average 2,000 people calling per day—quite a few more at Christmas—the crank and deviate calls are few and far between. The most innocent item in the catalogue can draw an exaggerated political response; when we first showed things from the People's Republic of China we were accused of selling out America and supporting the Communists. Our women are trained to ask once, "Are you ready to place your order?" then break the connection if someone is making an annoying call. They are told they do not have to listen to suggestive or obscene calls, and, if a customer is calling in a complaint and gets unreasonable, we have at all times a supervisor of the phone room who can either cool him off or get in touch with someone who can give him a swift, positive answer. Some of our specialists are marvelous. I listened for forty-five minutes once as a supervisor gradually soothed a woman in South Carolina who had returned a robe and had not received her refund check as quickly as she thought she should. The woman announced first that she had her lawyer on the other line, and then the lawyer began reading what sounded like an injunction, the gist of which was that Horchow would immediately cease and desist from taking any further orders or mailing any more refunds until this woman's check had reached her and been cleared by her bank.

At times like that, I tend to say, "All right . . ." just to get over the problem, but this supervisor handled it much better than that. Before she ended the episode, she not only had placated the woman and her lawyer, she had actually gotten another order out of the customer—and the customer guaranteed her the color, size, and specifications were correct and there would be no return. In fact, the woman herself said, "I'm so glad I didn't have to quit buying from your catalogue," and the lawyer asked to be put on our mailing list.

But I wouldn't try to pretend we settle all problems with irate customers so successfully. When there is an explanation, we try to offer them the reason something is delayed, why it might have arrived broken, or why it looks a little different in the cloth, perhaps, from the way it looked in the catalogue picture. We seldom have to go to the mat, as they say, with a customer, although sometimes a customer is mad enough to simply not want to hear an explanation, reasonable or not. So we do have an end to patience. If, in taking an order, it becomes apparent that the caller's idea of an item is grossly erroneous, we try to talk him out of placing the order with something like, "Perhaps this is not the item for you."

Every day we get mail orders with drawings of feet enclosed, or pieces of ribbon or string to indicate ring sizes. Several customers have asked that someone on our staff with the same size foot try on the shoe "and tell me if it's comfortable before I order." Or, "Let me try it on and if it's comfortable I'll pay then." There are also invariably a few dreamers who see some lovely gown or skirt in the catalogue and write, hopefully, "If a 12 runs large in that, maybe . . . I wear an 18 ordinarily."

When we went to a 24-hour telephone schedule, we did it mainly as a convenience to customers. We were prepared for those early morning hours barely to cover the cost of keeping the phone room in operation. Happily, that was not the case. We found, for one thing, that many people feel a sudden urge to buy from the catalogue while they are lounging before a midnight fire or sitting up reading because they can't sleep. The very first morning we were on our 24-hour telephone schedule we got a call from a Pacific coast state where the time was near 2 A.M. The woman said she'd been out to a party but wanted very badly to order a silver tea service. "I was taking off my dress and just happened to see your catalogue," she said, "and I knew if I waited until tomorrow I'd never order it." The order totaled something like $2,400 and our order taker wasn't sure it would still be wanted when a more sober awakening came, but it went through without a hitch, and I'm sure it was $2,400 we would never have seen if we hadn't been right there at the other end of a toll free call at two o'clock in the morning.

We have also discovered that a lot of entertainers and well-known persons like to order late at night. Sometimes they are just ending their work—finishing up a show at Las Vegas or on Broadway—or coming in from a party or a public appearance. It's about the only time they can call their own long enough to do some shopping. As some have explained, entertainers are basically night people by the nature of their work, and their lives are structured around their schedule, which is at odds with the rest of society.

Some of them also feel they have more privacy with a late call, privacy at their end of the line as well as ours.

Our telephone order takers are trained not to say things like,

"Is this *the* Miss Jones?" We certainly don't mind that they recognize famous names, and we don't mind them talking with the caller briefly on that basis, but we would never want to leave the impression that there is a "Miss Jones" who is more important to us than another "Miss Jones."

Most of the stars who call at night do so in person rather than having a secretary or a business manager do it. And, I am told, the stars ask pretty much the same questions concerning an item that Mrs. Muldoon of Memphis or Mr. Cooper of Cleburne might ask. They seldom want special favors, although I was surprised to learn, several years ago, that quite a few famous people do not use credit cards. It may be that they are afraid the cards will be used fraudulently, or maybe they feel that they are so well known they are entitled to credit wherever they shop, without a card. It can put a phone-order person on the spot, when a celebrity is on the line with a big order, and no credit card. One well-known male actor regularly demands that we discount the items we sell him because, he claims, "You'll use my name in your promotion." (Reading this, he will note that his name has not been used.)

One of the most fascinating hobbies of the order department is keeping a list of the unusual names that come in by mail and telephone. The fact that they are real names—we verify each one—adds to the interest. They are amusing, beautiful, rhyming, sonorous, ethereal. I particularly like first names with the musical quality of these: Serene, Dreama, Odlypso, Sweet, Tweet, Morning Star, Lightfoot, Psyche, Starlet, and Luster. Last names cover a variety of delightful areas, with such entries as: Darling, Happy, Tickle, Laughter, Fulilove, or Foote, Hand, Head, Shoulders, Arms, Finger, Nail, Legg, Chinn, and Bones. Not to mention Trout, Bass, Salmon, Perch, Pike, Ray, Turtle, Shark, Tuna, and Whale. We have Shakespeares and

Washingtons and Roosevelts and Jeffersons; we have Drags and Plunks and Zats; we have Silk, Wool, Cotton and Fabrik—and we have several James James, Jones Jones, Francis Francis, or Kennedy Kennedy, as well as Cash, Money, Bill, Penney, Nickle, and a few Halffs.

One thing that surprises me is how often a customer will rebel at the shipping charge but not the merchandise price. Beside each item in the catalogue is a figure in parentheses which represents the packing and shipping charge, *e.g.* (2.25). That figure represents an average on postage or United Parcel charges plus packing materials and preparation. We certainly don't try to do anything but break even on it, yet every day or so we get an indignant letter pointing out, "I paid $2.25 postage but when the package arrived it only had $1.95 on it: I want my 30 cents."

We try to explain that the parenthetical figure isn't the literal cost of postage alone, and that, for some items, an unusual amount of time and materials is needed for safe delivery, so the cost of packing alone can be more than our shipping charge, but with a few customers this discrepancy seems to count more than a mistake in price.

With orders coming in at a rate of thousands per week, complaints are bound to follow, even though they amount to a minor percentage of the flow. But it's especially important for a mail-order firm to pay the closest possible attention to complaints, even when the firm has good and reasonable answers. Mail-order companies, without visual contact, have the disadvantage of not being able to do the kind of face-to-face explaining that retail stores can do.

Aside from the "doesn't fit" and "arrived broken" complaints, we have discovered some inquiries that are standard throughout the mail-order industry.

- Premature delivery: We are asked to hold an order for a birthday or anniversary and it arrives early. Our explanation is that sometimes the shipping department fails to remember.
- When we describe a watch as having a 17-jewel movement, what kind of jewels are meant? Usually rubies, watchmakers say.
- Guarantee of others. Some products carry a separate guarantee by the maker or distributor but consumer complaints often come to us first. We try to do business only with manufacturers and suppliers who abide fully by their guarantee.
- Service companies. As with manufacturer guarantees, we often catch someone else's fallout.
- Sale goods. When we offer items at reduced price, we always get a few complaints that, "I paid full price for that last week." We try to explain that sale items are usually few in number and, as in a store's "after-holiday" sales, we don't know what is going to be reduced until we see what we have left.
- Forgetfulness. Sometimes we overlook something on an order, but, more often, the customer has forgotten what was ordered— or that it has been received already. This usually occurs when someone sees an entry on a credit card statement but can't recall what the item was, and, therefore, thinks it never arrived.
- Gift boxes cost too much. As with shipping charges, we only try to break even on gift boxes and wrap.
- The "Italian Handbag" incident. Once we offered a beautiful leather handbag which was described as "Italian" but was manufactured in Mexico even though designed by Italians. It was a mistake, because the public doesn't use the same vocabulary as the clothing and accessory industry, where our phrase would have been accepted. We now use phrases such as "Italian-styled" or "Scandinavian-inspired" and have a letter explaining such usage if a customer complains.
- "You Texans!" Sometimes we are blamed for things that have nothing to do with the Horchow organization because of our location. Myths of geography are hard to defend against.

Surprisingly enough, the one major item to be returned to us is the man's necktie. Apparel in general has the highest rate of returns, as might be expected. Colors aren't always seen the same from one pair of eyes to the next, and color definitions are, at best, imprecise.

The most ridiculous accusation made against me (I took it quite personally) was that the Horchow catalogue "exploited children." I held onto my angry impulses and replied that either a few of the children pictured in the Horchow catalogue had been, in fact, my own; or, they were the children of friends and company officials who were pleased to be included as models; or, they were paid models from an agency—and paid well.

Every operation also receives "carbon-copy protests" from self-appointed individuals or groups who flood the mails without investigating whether the person or firm they are attacking is doing any of the things they claim to be outraged over. For example, we have donated many thousands of dollars toward valid environmental and ecological projects around the globe, yet I continue to get nasty letters from ill-informed persons asserting their ecological sensitivity and misunderstanding something they see in our catalogue—or, frequently, from people who haven't even looked at our catalogue. I have even gotten letters protesting Ultrasuede (which is synthetic) because some people seem to think it is leather and that anything made of leather comes from an endangered species. We do not offer anything derived from an endangered species.

I have also gotten scurrilous letters accusing me of every shade of racism and every kind of political dogma, including several letters which took it for granted we were secret Red Agents because the Horchow Collection was one of the first catalogues in the United States to offer a substantial range of merchandise from the People's Republic of China. It is sad that many good causes and concerns are damaged by blind zeal—or is it a form of hatred? Also, as a merchant, I am weary of those who think we are making (or ought to make) a social statement every time we print a catalogue.

XX

Learning to Live With the Scams

ONE OF THE MAJOR keys to success in the mail-order business is the credit card. It is the very foundation of our telephone-ordering section, because, without the international credit card, this type of selling would be virtually impossible.

But the credit card can also be a villain. It leads to more fraud and theft than almost anything invented by the modern mind except the computer. Attempted theft by credit card is one of our biggest problems, and we have developed a department of sleuths that is part of a large network working to guard firms against this kind of loss.

The main source of trouble is that a credit card is, in itself, a guarantee that someone has a certain amount of credit. But who? It's bad enough in an establishment where the one presenting the card can be seen in person and other kinds of identification can be requested. Those credit card swindles one reads about where some person, or couple, passes through fifteen or twenty states collecting staggering amounts of merchandise, nearly always take place in person. Mail-order card theft may be as big on a cumulative basis, but it would take an extraordinary number of "hits" to run up an enormous score on any single catalogue, because unusually large orders get intensive research and very few bad orders slip through.

Most attempts at credit-card fraud are opportunistic; someone finds a copy of a valid credit-card transaction and decides to use the name and number on the spur of the moment. It isn't difficult to come up with a carbon copy (a flimsy) of a credit-card transaction. At this point, it seems an unbreakable national bad habit to wad them up and toss them away or just to stick them in the glove compartment of the auto.

The temptation to use them fraudulently on a telephone order is overwhelming to some people who find copies, especially if they have also found a copy of a mail-order catalogue. Something clicks, and, next thing, they're on the phone, ordering everything they see that excites them. These are the easy ones to spot. If for no other reason, they're too easy to please. An order taker says, "We're out of that," or, "We don't have that size," and the would-be con artist quickly amends the order or says, "Oh, if you're out of size 9s, send me two 14s." Our people are downright canny at spotting this kind of thing, but we can't afford to make our suspicions too plain, because not all easy-to-please callers are trying to rip us off. So we never make a direct accusation. We have a set of questions we ask on every order and these questions are, in themselves, adequate to turn back the casually larcenous. For one thing, we ask the telephone number, the shipping address, and sometimes the office phone number. This is for the protection of the cardholder as well as to make verification easier.

Professionals are another matter. They, too, generally prefer using a flimsy rather than an actual card because the unsuspecting cardholder, knowing his credit card is "safe" in his purse or wallet, won't find out for several weeks that he's been victimized. Quite often, in fact, our phone-order department will be the first to alert the legitimate cardholder that someone is trying to defraud, and, with luck, this will be the first attempt.

Sometimes a card is stolen and an address forged, and for a short time quite a few orders can go to that fake address. But, here again, it is only a matter of a few days before someone up or down the identification chain gets wise. We have had some deliverymen refuse to take packages to certain addresses because they know (from being at the site) that some kind of ring is operating there.

Through the years we have had trouble with several rings in Chicago, New York, Detroit, and the Los Angeles area. (It is usually in a big city or its suburbs.) Suddenly we get many orders from different names going to the same address, or we get several orders from the same name going to different addresses. Thanks to the computer we have "black lists" of certain postal zones, certain addresses in certain cities, and certain names. An order involving any of these is automatically kicked out for closer inspection and checking.

There is one zip code in Virginia to which we simply do not ship. It is a correctional institution which seems to offer such independence to its inmates that the authorities have no control over what goes out or comes in. Apparently, the inmates are able (surreptitiously, of course) to print up very legitimate-looking business letterheads, duplicate bank checks, and obtain valid credit-card numbers and names—or anything else they need to use to swindle "the outside." It was on the advice of the prison authorities that we totally cut off that zip code. That was the only solution they could offer.

Unfortunately for those in prison who are attempting to straighten out their lives, prisons are a constant source of trouble to mail-order firms. Maybe it has to do with the feeling that nothing further can be done to a miscreant, or sometimes it may be the work of an intelligent, imaginative mind with nothing else to do. Also, if you wanted to operate a "scam," where could you go to find more experts?

Not all prisons are as mildly controlled as the Virginia institution I mentioned. Some prisons do not allow prisoners to receive packages or engage in commercial transactions, as I found out a few years back. I received a letter from a man who said he was serving a life term in a western prison. He wanted to give a Christmas present to his lawyer, he wrote, and asked if he might send a small amount each month until he had accumulated enough to cover an item in our catalogue. I accepted his proposal, and he began to send a few dollars at a time until he had about $30 with us.

That June I was interviewed by *The Wall Street Journal* and I mentioned this unusual customer. The reporter wrote: "Catalogue readers say they enjoy the convenience of shopping at home, as opposed to coping with throngs . . . others have little choice. One client of the Horchow Collection is a man on the West Coast who's in prison for life. Even though the attorney lost his case, he wants to show his appreciation to his lawyer. So, periodically, he sends Horchow $10 as part of a layaway plan to buy the attorney a gift, as yet unselected."

Within a matter of days I received a hot letter from the lifer saying he thought he would sue me, for I had betrayed his confidence, and demanding I return his money. That prison must have an interesting library, to get both the Horchow Collection catalogue and *The Wall Street Journal.*

Professional swindlers don't fool with dresses or apparel. They order watches, jewelry, television sets—the higher priced, quickly-disposed-of items. A theft ring in California (we suspect it was a family) didn't follow this pattern. Using different addresses, certain ring members kept ordering pages and pages of everything and anything. Even after we had long since refused to ship, the members kept ordering. We finally decided the women and girls wanted the clothing, the men wanted the high-ticket goods, and cousins or whoever would get the rest as gifts. A lot of swindlers keep on trying, even after we have discovered their fake orders, addresses, or numbers. I suppose they are just playing the odds, hoping sooner or later an order will slip through. And, of course, it's hard to track down a fraudulent order, once it's dispatched, so they feel safe. The computer, with its detailed multimillion memory, does a good job of protecting us.

Something most readers don't realize is that when a mail-order firm is defrauded by credit card, the firm is the loser, not the credit-card company. They charge all the fake tickets back to us, so there's no faceless moneyman out there absorbing the loss. Under the circumstances of a mail- or phone-order sale, we can't get the same protection a retail transaction has. We can't check signatures or demand other forms of identification, so our only real protection is not to ship.

Sometimes it becomes difficult to be certain an order is fraudulent. We do not make direct accusations, because, even when our suspicions are aroused, fraud is not always the case. There is also the delicate problem of children ordering without permission on parents' cards, of mentally retarded or emotionally upset people making calls, or of senile folks who forget their names and addresses, or why they were calling, while they are still on the phone to us. A good many customers have nervous phone habits, stumbling over the names of gift recipients who are sisters, brothers, or close friends. And we also have an occasional real customer who lives in a "black-listed" zip-code area.

On top of everything else, unless we have an actual loss—

having delivered something to a false cardholder or a swindler of some other sort—we can't prosecute. However, I don't want to create any false hope in larcenous hearts. We have an excellent track record in convicting the professionals and the rings. There is a tremendous amount of cooperation between the mail-order firms, the U.S. Postal Service, the banks, the card companies, and the United Parcel Service or other private delivery services.

Brazen is the word for some fake orders. Take one we hovered over for months in 1978. We received an order for two very expensive Cartier watches, with a name and a valid credit-card number that checked out. However, something about the order caught the ear of our telephone order taker—something about the way the voice hesitated, maybe, or the slightest sort of discrepancy in spelling. The supervisor, on consultation, decided that on an order of this size a little caution might pay off. She called the telephone number given and was assured by a voice on the other end (in New York) that the order was valid. In fact, the voice chided, why weren't the watches already there ... they were to be presented as Christmas gifts.

The supervisor still wasn't satisfied. Overly insistent customers naturally arouse a sixth sense of doubt. The supervisor checked a New York crisscross directory and found the number was an office in a world-famous organization. She called the organization switchboard and asked for Mr. K, who supposedly had placed the order. She was told that Mr. K, a high official, was in Asia.

This was red-alert. A hold was immediately put on the order for the watches, but, even though our sleuths were, by now, tingling with suspicion, there was still a chance of a mistake being made. Then we got another call from New York. An angry voice identified itself as Mr. K and demanded, "Where are the watches I ordered? My patience has just about run out."

Our sleuth replied, "But Mr. K, you're supposed to be in Calcutta."

There was only slight hesitation if any. "I flew back in for a world conference."

Well, we went back and forth with Mr. K or whoever was trying to use his credit card. First, he had just arrived back in New York, then he had just gone away again. Once he was back in New York, he insisted, on a secret mission which even the organization didn't know about. But every time he called he demanded his two Cartier watches. We could never prove our customer was not the real Mr. K because we could never get in touch with anyone else who could convince us he was. Apparently, the true Mr. K was as much a global hedge-hopper as the false one claimed he was.

Although the world organization was above question, and presumably Mr. K, too, we decided there was a veritable network of swindlers within the office, whose members were able to keep one jump ahead of us by way of the telephone—and yet, we didn't dare send investigators to check out the situation because we didn't know whom to investigate. Despite the fact that the interloper called to file phony complaints, we couldn't pinpoint who it was. We did not ship, and, after several months, we were assured that the real Mr. K had not ordered the watches.

The persistency of some swindlers amounts to unbelievable gall. They can sound utterly convincing as they storm and protest, even when we know very well they are as fake as the names they're trying to pass with. They threaten to sic Betty Furness on us, they use legitimate letterheads or beautifully engraved false ones, some trying to set up corporate accounts with us using such tricks. Now and then someone uses a celebrity name, saying he or she is a brother or sister (or mother) of the celebrity. Sometimes they will call an order half a dozen times, even after we have made it plain we are not going to ship. To date, we have never refused to ship to a legitimate customer, so we feel pretty safe when we finally reach the point that we have to tell someone, "Nothing doing."

Also, there is a class of people who, perhaps, are not trying to defraud but who don't get shipped. One man seems to travel all over Europe, mailing orders from Paris, Berlin, Zurich, Rome, wherever he happens to spend a few days. He encloses personal checks written on a bank in whatever city he's favoring, and sometimes a descriptive folder from a hotel or nearby resort. I'm really sorry to say that none of his checks has ever been good, so, of course, none of his orders has ever been filled.

We never reject an order because of the form it is written on. We get all kinds of other mail-order companies' order forms with their names scratched out and "Horchow" written in. Other customers use some astonishing pieces of paper to write orders on. Almost any day will see one written on the back of a grocery list, a prescription, a bank-deposit slip, or a blank check, and pages from personal letters are not uncommon. Our all-time winner in this category is one sheet of a letter from a man (married) to his mistress. The mistress appears, from the letter, to be the wife of either a golfing companion or his boss—or both. This is truly an uncommon order form.

One summer a postman saved us several hundred dollars. A team of professional thieves discovered a wealthy couple, who lived in a large apartment building, was going on a round-the-world tour. The pros set up a "drop," using another apartment number in the same building, and began using the stolen credit cards of the couple to place substantial orders with us and other mail firms. But, as luck would have it, the parcel-post man recognized the names and, knowing the couple's apartment number, changed every one of the fake numbers to the real one. When the couple arrived back in the U.S. after a three-month absence, their apartment was full of packages they hadn't ordered. They were furious, but, when their business manager phoned to demand an explanation, the scheme became immediately apparent. To show how well the pros had planned, this couple's charge accounts were paid automatically each month by the business manager, so only after their return did he discover they had not ordered the things. Even the card companies hadn't found out what was happening.

Mail orders are easier than phone orders to keep "clean," but, when fraudulent orders do come in, we have order takers who can recognize faked signatures or black-listed addresses, and can even spot "guilty" typewriters—those that have been used on fake orders in the past—out of the thousands of orders that pour in each day. One of the simplest safeguards, although it's out of our hands when it happens, is the undeliverable package. Someone slips a fraudulent order through but, in the meantime, for some reason or from cold feet, he isn't there to claim the package—or the address turns out to be a burned-out building. And our suspicious sleuths have been known not only to stop an order on the packing line, they've run out to the UPS or parcel-post truck and taken something off as the truck is pulling away from our dock. Under certain conditions, we have even stopped delivery after a package has reached its city of destination.

We have relatively few problems with personal checks. Our check checkers know just about every bank in North America, including a few which still do not use magnetic ink character recognition numbers on the face of the check. That means these banks' customers can, and some do, write checks on just any kind of substance they pick up that will carry writing. And some personal checking accounts are in fanciful names, like "Dimpled Darling" or "Nuts and Bolts." The authorized signatures for these accounts are, in themselves, often works of art. One customer signs his name backwards on his checks. Our signature may be the last place we can truly show our creative side. Just so it clears the bank.

XXI

The Crystal Ball Meets the Computer

THE WAVE OF MAIL-order catalogues flooding American mailboxes has crested. I think 1978 probably saw the largest number of people in the business or trying to get in the business. Many people apparently thought mail order was a wonderful thing to do—why, you could start it right in your kitchen or use the dining room table—so they tried it. But, if that approach ever worked (and I doubt that it did), it won't work anymore. I have said (and I have clippings to prove it) I wished anyone well who entered the mail-order business, and, if they could get the orders, more power to them. I wouldn't be writing this book if competition scared me. But the shakedown in the catalogue field began some time ago. There are a number of catalogues I don't see now, and there were a number of new ones I never saw again after the first mailing.

I was flattered when, in a 1978 newsletter, the National Society of Mail Retailers warned: "The proliferation of catalogues trying to imitate the Horchow Collection and Neiman–Marcus probably is going to result in one of the biggest washouts ever seen . . . but it's as inevitable as night following day. You can't build a successful business by saying, 'Look, he did it. Why can't we do it, too?' "

This doesn't mean the mail-order business itself is going to slow down. Modern high-end mail order, as contrasted to the traditional catalogue houses, has taken over too large a place in retail trade for that to happen. Modern mail order might be compared, however, to a new invention emerging in industry, or something like television. At first there were dozens, even hundreds, of brands and makes offered, then, as the industry gained experience, the number of makers shrank even as the number of sets sold expanded enormously. Jac Vroom, who is now a mail-order consultant, says, "The luxury catalogue *idea* isn't the 'message' anymore. It's the implementation of the idea that now brings success, or survival; the next generation of ideas will take over."

I see more participation by major stores in the catalogue business. "Let's have a mail-order catalogue that's separate from the store," they will say, and copy what we've done or what Neiman–Marcus has done. In fact, Neiman–Marcus, in 1978, finally started "N–M by Post," a separate mail-order division with merchandise that can be bought only by mail—as I tried to get the store to do in the late 1960s. The chains are beginning to realize you can get lots of extra business from customers who never come to your store.

Mail order at the so-called luxury level has the same innovative potential that the convenience stores had in the 1940s and 1950s. They offered a modest stock, but they stayed open when the larger stores were closed, and they were located within a short distance of your home. Today they do a huge percentage of national retail food sales even though competing with the supermarkets. The reason is in the name: convenience.

The same thing is happening to mail order, and I believe it will occupy a larger and larger place in everybody's life. Once a consumer tries mail order a few times it becomes not just a habit but a way of life. Not only is it more convenient, it will offer items not found elsewhere and present opportunities to get things you didn't know existed. And in some cases the mail-order catalogue helps you make up your mind by editing the merchandise before presenting it, at prices comparable to those of the stores.

I have had people ask me if I'm not afraid to make the mail-order business sound too rosy. I'm not, because not just anyone who gets into it is going to find it rosy or is going to stay. You can't succeed in the business unless you have a purpose for being in it. Good taste and pretty pictures aren't enough. Also, as the newsletter warned, you cannot merely copy someone who is successful.

For the merchandising community, mail order is the most exciting frontier there is. A friend, seeing my name in several magazine articles at the same time, wrote me, "You're in a hot industry and they can't write an article about that industry without mentioning you." I'm proud to be linked so closely to the industry, and my pal was right, it is *the* hot industry. Everyone seems to be discovering this at once. *Time* magazine had two articles on shopping by mail in one month, *Forbes* had a piece on me, and there was a flood of articles about doing Christmas dinner by mail, trimming the tree by mail, outfitting the whole family by mail—and numerous confessions of catalogue "junkies" in a score of metropolitan newspapers. One of them wrote, after giving her order to the Horchow telephone operator, "You know, I feel like I've just been talking to Santa Claus."

* * *

Despite my feeling that mail order is the brightest star in the retail firmament, it will not remain the way it has been. As one of the other catalogue producers told *Women's Wear Daily* some time ago, "Catalogues, not joggers, are the new urban blight."

Dollar volume of mail-order business will continue to increase, but good profits will be tougher and tougher to get as the quality of competition increases. For instance, operating under the same business rules as we had in the past, in 1978 we had a big increase in sales but profits declined almost as much as sales grew. Why? Well, nothing about the mail-order business is getting any cheaper. Mail and delivery rates never seem to stop climbing, paper and printing costs increase every year, and catalogue production figures, such as photography, artwork, copywriting, and modeling fees, keep pace. When you add in the national and international inflation rate currently afflicting the trade world, you arrive at the situation described in *Alice in Wonderland*, where you have to run very hard to stay in the same place.

But the real profit measure is less nebulous. It is called customer response per thousands of catalogues mailed. In general terms, it is the ratio of catalogue sales to catalogue costs, in number of orders, number of items per order, and number of dollars. The cost of the catalogue is the biggest expense outside the cost of the merchandise itself. We aim for 5 cents, after taxes, as our profit goal. After merchandise costs of 50 cents, operations costs of 10 cents, fixed overhead of 6 cents, and taxes of 5 cents, that used to leave us with approximately 24 cents to pay for the catalogue. Unfortunately, the cost of the catalogue has climbed to 31, 32, and 33 cents per copy, delivered to your mailbox. At this margin, when customer response per thousand catalogues drops, profit is eliminated, and, if returns from customers go up even 1 percent, you can be crippled. And, if you can't find a way to increase customer response—get each customer to order more items, order more often, or spend more dollars per order—you may have to leave the party without eating dessert.

The mail-order business will undoubtedly use advanced technology to make more profit from sales. The computer made possible modern mail order, and the credit card made possible the telephone phase of it, so there are bound to be future steps taken which will cut down on one or more of the costs I have outlined. One such advance may involve the presentation of the catalogue itself. At some point we will have television presentation of goods, via cable, perhaps, where a beautiful woman or handsome man will model, or will describe items, offering them one at a time while you sit in your living room or bedroom and punch a push-button phone or some other kind of registering device which will order what you want in color, size, and numbers you desire. Everything will be automatic, including a credit check, and, after a period of time in which you will be allowed to change the data—or change your mind—your order will begin moving to you in something like five or ten seconds after you push the final selector.

That system is not only possible right now, it is in use on an experimental basis in some cities. But the transmission of goods is still in the hands of the U.S. Postal Service and the private delivery agencies, so it still takes about the same length of time as it did many years ago for delivery of a package from point A to point B. An electronic ordering system would cut a day or two off the time an order is received, processed, and sent out, but getting it to the customer is still going to eat up the major portion of elapsed time. Once such an electronic system is installed, it will certainly save the mail-order firms money, but the system will have to be nationwide to be effective, and I don't see anything national on the horizon at present.

One facet of electronic ordering we have been waiting for since the early 1950s is the television telephone. Here, again, the advantage would be primarily in speeding up ordering and credit checks. Having visual contact with a customer would also eliminate some delay because our operators would be able to hold up something to the transmitter and the customer could inspect it on the video display in her home. But getting the item there would remain the biggest time-consuming step, and, once again, Uncle Sam or the package services would control the calendar.

I anticipate the use of credit cards will be enhanced in a short time. We've been waiting for video telephones for more than a quarter century, but a credit-card verification system should easily beat that timetable. With it you may insert your card, possibly punching a secret code number on your telephone, and have your order entered into the computer in a matter of seconds. Credit cards are already used to extract cash from machines at all hours and in many locations—why not arrange for them to do the same thing on a national credit network?

I believe the greatest forward steps in mail-order business operations will be more mechanized fulfillment systems. With the advancement of this concept, you will ultimately place an order directly to a computer which will be able to talk to you—a system already functioning at Bell Telephone. The computer will handle such customer services as returns, wrong sizes, and breakages. Personally, I would always want a friendly ear somewhere in the system to listen to those unusual gripes or other thoughts the customer might have. Even with a direct, computerized, order-taking system I think I would insist on building in some spot-response tapes with a few seconds of local weather, perhaps, or a friendly question for the human caller to answer.

Off in the future we may see a new kind of transportation

system which will enable the transmission of goods almost instantly. After all, the rail network of the world was nonexistent before the nineteenth century, and the jet airplanes that bring global cities within hours of each other only began commercial work in 1957. Who's to say that rocket shipping is another century away?

The Horchow Collection is already changing with the demands of its clientele. Our growth has been fast, but I like change and feel it is almost always good. We were the first catalogue to be issued independent of a store, offering a general line of higher-priced, fashion-keyed apparel, gifts, and useful items. Neiman–Marcus pioneered the catalogue-as-work-of-art with its Christmas books and their "His and Her" gifts, but, as Stanley Marcus has written in *House Beautiful*, "Little did we realize that we were starting something that would bring publicity and renown to our store beyond our wildest imagination." I modestly propose that as a result of my experience at that store I was inspired to take the idea several steps further and help make the luxury mail-order business the hot industry it has become.

I picked up lots of competitors, or, I should say, my idea picked up lots of competitors. And lots of imitators. Does that competition hurt? Of course, it hurts in the general way that losing "firstness" in any field hurts a business. But, in the case of the Horchow Collection, it hurts only because we can't have things quite as uncomplicated again.

We have never waited for the rest of the mail-order business to catch up with us, though, or to come up with something before we do. We have tried to be careful charting our changes, because I like change for its own sake sometimes, and this can be dangerous. I have been candid in describing the flops and failures of change, and one lesson we have learned about them is that we always need to digest growth. In the mail-order business you don't survive on growth, you survive on control. This means that every so often, after a season of unusual growth, you have to pull back. Digest. For instance, we used to mail millions of catalogues a year, using every name we could get our hands on. Experience has taught us that half a million catalogues can do the same job, if we preselect our targets.

A bad economy seems to have more effect on a store than on the mail-order business. Part of the reason is that when you go into a store in person you are making yourself vulnerable to overspending; the salesperson, just by being there, tends to make you feel bad because you aren't buying more. From a catalogue, you can budget spending and exercise all the restraint you need.

Another factor in mail-order growth is that more and more people hold jobs; thus, the public just doesn't have as much time to shop. Sure, many stores stay open on certain nights of the week, and some are open all night, but retail shopping remains basically a nine-to-five activity in the United States. Mail order never closes and it can go wherever the customer wants to go. Regardless of the comparative levels of efficiency among postal systems, the mail generally *does* go through. We get orders from all over the world, both from local residents and from American or Canadian citizens who might be visiting. We even continued to get orders from Iran during the darkest weeks of that country's revolution.

When I speak of the catalogues that have disappeared or others which have failed to gain follow-the-leader success, I am talking primarily about the general catalogues, not the specialty books which include only certain things, such as tools or maritime items. These specialty firms have a different market in mind and, for the most part, have little competition, although that doesn't make their job any easier. A few specialty books, like those that feature foods and kitchenwares, do face lots of others in their field.

Conglomerates have taken over a number of famous catalogues. For example, General Mills owns Eddie Bauer and Parker Pen Company owns Norm Thompson. Conglomerates will take over several more mail-order firms if the industry remains as attractive as it was in the 1970s. But conglomerate ownership isn't anything to fear if your firm is well established and has the innovativeness to stay in front of the changing field. Just as the catalogue section of a big retail chain must be independent, the catalogue operations of a conglomerate should be separate from any other division. One advantage private ownership has over conglomerate management is the ability to change quickly, to move in a new direction as soon as a move is indicated. Big stores can't do it for a number of reasons—and conglomerate ownership fails in this, too. First, few stores or chains are run by one person, and, if they are controlled by an individual, that individual isn't usually broadly trained to understand the problems and potentials of every division. The chief executive officer may be a specialist, but that specialty will almost always be either in law, taxation, or whatever is the biggest moneymaker of the assembled companies. That isn't ordinarily the mail-order company.

I know from experience that economic influence and input within the big stores is always changing, and with these changes comes changing philosophy—especially when it comes to producing and mailing a catalogue. One year jewelry will need to have the lead, the next it may be apparel, or maybe the head of the giftwares gets very determined about how his section should be represented. That is one reason it has taken so long for the chains to separate their mail-order business from store business. The catalogue director has to take orders—not always wise ones—from the store's income leader of the moment.

Also, did you ever stop to think that if you went from city to city shopping at the famous-name stores, you would find pretty much the same lines and merchandise? Of course, stores like Bloomingdale's, Neiman–Marcus, or Lord & Taylor will have their special boutiques, exclusive lines, and house labels, but they will offer very similar things—and quite often will offer the same brand names or the same designer clothes. So, if a store gets into mail order on a large scale, a change in merchandising philosophy will have to take place or the catalogue will read pretty much the same as those of the other stores.

Over 400,000 persons answered our little magazine ads in 1978 and asked that the Horchow Collection catalogue be sent to them. At the time, we already had a list of 1.2 million names to whom we mailed catalogues. But the heart of our list is not the number of names, it is proven responders. Of those 400,000 new names and those 1.2 million others, only a certain percentage will buy, or will continue to buy, for any length of time. Our problem is to keep a healthy balance—about one million—of buying customers. We need to find out what they want and what they're tired of, and keep their response climbing. We usually add to our mailing list the names of gift recipients unless they are already on it. Sometimes the recipients aren't human beings; people often order gifts in the name of their pet. Consequently, we have gotten letters saying, "Please quit sending my dog a catalogue," or, "My cat McCarthy can't read but he complains you never offer mice." One letter, from a five-year-old Irish setter in Hawaii, began, "I can't begin to tell you how pleased you made me by placing me on the Horchow mailing list." (We also got a glowing letter from a squirrel one autumn when we featured a squirrel on the cover of our catalogue.)

I don't want more and more growth because I don't want to have to do the things that a great deal more growth forces me to do. When a catalogue's sales get really big, the company must turn more and more to mass production goods. This means such a catalogue will have fewer and fewer "discoveries" of the delightful sort a buyer might turn up in a faraway bazaar or on an American Indian reservation. Handmade or hand-assembled goods can't be merchandised on the grand scale because they can't be produced on the grand scale. I want to digest, and part of this process is to keep that customer list at a solid one million. The attrition rate runs about 10 percent per year, and our effectiveness date (the point when our customer last ordered from us) cuts off another percentage, so we need to add nearly 20 percent new names to our buyers' list each year.

I have asked our customers what they want from Horchow and they have answered, "More things to buy." We asked, "What things?" and some told me they would like to buy books, so we set up a Horchow book club in 1979. In 1977 customers told me they would be interested in a Horchow fragrance line, so we introduced L'Envoi, which means (appropriately enough) "The sending." I was prepared for success, but was overwhelmed at the reception L'Envoi got. Without ever having smelled one whiff of the delightful violet-rose-jasmine-musk fragrance, thousands of customers ordered the perfume or cologne, making it a major American scent within two months of its introduction. We have since included samples of L'Envoi in thousands of outgoing orders, but its success was assured by the time most of our catalogue customers got their samples.

What I see in the future of mail order is an operation somewhat like a big shopping mall. There are all kinds of things that can be offered. Anything can be sold by mail—pianos, automobiles—remember our elephant story? Several companies sell *houses* by mail. I see this mail-order "mall" anchored at each end by a general store with specialty shops in between. In our own operation the Horchow catalogue will always be the cornerstone, but our Trifles catalogue has proven to be an exceptionally successful book and has created its own set of customers—just as it now has its own set of buyers, its own telephone-order numbers, and its own mailing list. We will probably find other catalogue ideas to work with, such as specialty and "new trend" books.

In 1979 we purposely cut down on apparel in our catalogues for the simple reason that while it accounts for 60 percent of our returns from customers, it only accounts for 22 percent of our sales. But that doesn't mean we would ever cut off apparel completely, and it doesn't mean we might not send out a special apparel book if a way around high returns, fashion changes, and seasonal obsolescence can succeed. Apparel needs a quicker outlet. You can't hold a dress over until next fall because it will be either out of fashion or done to death in the stores. Having to buy two seasons ahead for the catalogue is bad enough, and you have to face the fact you're going to carry a lot over because you can't get a fast reshipment to take care of unexpected demands. In women's clothing, nothing is wanted if the season is waning or ended, even if some dress or skirt was a best-seller.

This brings up the matter of taste. I have been asked to lecture and write about taste both by people in the industry and by people outside the industry who hope I can give them some infallible secret for making a tasteful choice every time. I feel that taste is a matter of two things: use and proportion. I believe a tasteful object is usually useful and simple. It may contain an intricate pattern, or be ornamented with complex designs, but their proportions and their purpose will make some kind of artistic or intrinsic sense. In the end, excellence will characterize good taste. Too often we confuse *taste* and *style.* Style comes and goes (although there is good taste even within styles), but taste must be applied first. I have not found a way to discover if my buyers have taste, for instance. I only look at the things they buy and judge them on their excellence. Not everything we offer appeals to everyone, and certainly if you don't like something in a Horchow catalogue it doesn't mean you have poor taste. But I sincerely believe we have not offered anything in poor taste in any of our books.

As I've mentioned, we have established several Horchow Collection Finale stores—at this writing only in Texas—and may plan others in major population centers. Our Finale stores offer at substantial discounts goods which are no longer in the catalogue. Sometimes the Finale will have only a few of some item and sometimes (I hate to admit) it will have a few hundred, if we overestimated our catalogue sales. We have found that customers truly *love* the Finale stores, some of them coming in two or three times a week to see what new item is for sale—because of the low prices, some items sell out almost as soon as we display them. We have also found that a large number of Finale customers are *not* mail-order customers.

Our outlet store idea will be picked up by competitors, I am sure, so it ranks as another important innovation the industry learned from us. We have, of course, continued to offer special mail sales and sale catalogues so that everyone, whether near a Horchow Finale store or not, can have the same chance to pick up bargains.

Another area of transition in the mail-order business is the catalogues themselves. Gucci charges $5 for its catalogue and there was one mail-order company you had to become a member of to be allowed to order. Now that postage, printing, and paper are becoming so high that it will soon cost $1 or more to produce a catalogue, we have had to limit the number of people to whom we send books.

We're not mailing catalogues to a million random names anymore, only to some 600,000 of the most recent buyers. I can see the time coming when we'll mail the nonsteady buyers only the Christmas catalogue. In other words, we're condensing our list, not just to cut people off but because some of you don't need, or want, every catalogue we mail, and you've told us so. But if someone writes who hasn't bought anything in, say, three or four years and says, "Why don't I get a catalogue?" we'll mail it again.

We have to figure out ways to be sure we are mailing to the most productive part of the list, and to find other ways to get people to buy. Our Horchow Book Society list is not nearly so extensive as our general gift list and is not duplicated, in many cases. If we develop other special catalogues in the future, they will not, in all probability, go to even as many as half our general list. They will go only to the ones who have indicated they are interested in whatever the special catalogue offers.

But mailing a catalogue is like opening a store: You don't just open your store for business on the first and fifteenth of the month. You open your store as often as people want to buy, and you ask them, "What else would you like to have?" You keep finding ways to solicit their business, and, if you have some skill and luck, pretty soon you are opening your store every day.

What I want to do is have a stable core of a million customers. I want to be sure that I nurture them, that I correspond with them, that they buy more and more often and buy more and more merchandise—because they like it and find it handy . . . and find it only through me. I want to make this million my universe and not worry constantly about adding more and more worlds to it—just maintain that core of about a million friends.

Because, if I can maintain a million friends, from old and new names and faces, I can always keep going.

Index